MYSTICISM, FREUDIANISM

AND

SCIENTIFIC PSYCHOLOGY

MYSTICISM, FREUDIANISM

AND

SCIENTIFIC PSYCHOLOGY

BY

KNIGHT DUNLAP

BOOKS FOR LIBRARIES PRESS
FREEPORT, NEW YORK

First Published 1920
Reprinted 1971

INTERNATIONAL STANDARD BOOK NUMBER:
0-8369-5838-1

LIBRARY OF CONGRESS CATALOG CARD NUMBER:
79-160970

PRINTED IN THE UNITED STATES OF AMERICA

TO

MORTON PRINCE

Principi in Psychopathologia Americana

PREFACE

The past decade has witnessed a remarkable revival of popular interest in philosophical mysticism and in spiritualism. Along with this revival has gone a spread of the so-called "newer psychology" of Freud and his satellites, which, beginning in the medical field, now claims the whole arena of human activities. The spiritualistic developments have been, by various authors, attributed to the war; and perhaps the war, with its profound mental and spiritual upheavals, may have contributed to them. The simultaneous developments in the hoary cult of philosophical mysticism, and the newer cult of Freudianism nevertheless indicate that the movements have derived their impetus only in small part from the events of the last few years, but are the expressions of forces which have been much longer in their releasing, and depend on deeply implanted principles of human nature.

To show that it is no mere curious accident which leads booksellers to shelve together books on these three topics, is in part the purpose of the present volume. The fact that patrons who look over the stock on one of these subjects are apt to be interested in the others, has its foundation in the real unity of the three, which runs through their diversities. And all three involve an assault on the very life of the biological sciences; an assault which scientific psychology alone is capable of warding off. In implicit recognition of this fact, each makes its immediate attack on the methods and results of scientific psychology. Hence it is the duty of the psychologist to enlighten the public concerning the real nature of this siren trinity.

I had projected the inclusion in this volume of a study of spiritualism, along with that of mysticism and psychoanalysis. But the adequate treatment of spiritualism really requires a volume to itself, and is not essential to the discussion of Freudianism, although it illuminates the latter. Moreover, spiritualism makes its maximal appeal to a part of the public which differs from that to which psychoanalysis is most attractive; its antagonism to science is more open and undisguised. Psychoanalysis, which attempts to creep in wearing the uniform of science, and to strangle it from the inside, is the more immediate danger, and spiritualism may be allowed to wait.

I hope in a later volume to analyze the phenomena on which spiritualism is built, and point out the commonplace psychological principles on which they may be explained. In the same volume also, I plan to give a full exposition of the phenomena and causes of dreams.

I may here record my opinion that the final result of the Freudian movement may be beneficial, although the immediate effects are the deluding of many persons, and the temporary checking of psychological research. Just as Christian Science has tremendously accelerated the progress of Scientific Medicine, so psychoanalysis, by compelling psychology to put its own house in order, will eventually help in the development of the Scientific Psychology it aims to thrust aside.

The constructive third part, on the Foundations of Scientific Psychology, was included at the suggestion of Dr. Buford Johnson, to whose critical assistance is due in great measure such coherence as this volume may have. I am very much indebted also to Professor W. D. Furry for his careful and capable revision of the proof.

KNIGHT DUNLAP.

Baltimore, August, 1920.

CONTENTS

CHAPTER I

CHAPTER II

CHAPTER III

12   *Contents*

MYSTICISM, FREUDIANISM AND SCIENTIFIC PSYCHOLOGY

CHAPTER I

MYSTICISM

The term *mysticism* and its cognate terms *mystical* and *mystic* have in popular usage a range of somewhat confusing meanings. In the technical language of philosophy, however, these terms have a definite application to a specific doctrine of knowledge: and it is with this narrow and proper significance of the terms that we are here concerned. The words themselves are derived from the Greek word *mysterion* which means a "secret religious ceremony." "Mysterion" in turn is derived from the word *myo* which means "to be mysterious or secret;" literally, "to keep one's mouth shut." "Mysterious" and "mystery" are from the same word from which these other terms are derived. Originally a "mystery" was something which should be kept secret, which one could not reveal. In modern usage, however, a "mystery" is merely something about which one cannot learn the truth. "Mysterious" is the adjective cognate with "mystery;'' and ''mystic'' as an adjective belongs with these two terms. ''Mystic'' as a noun, means one who holds the doctrine which is called ''mysticism,'' or who practically applies some of the results of that doctrine.

Mysticism may be defined briefly in a well established phrase as *the belief in a third kind of knowledge.* It has played so important a part in the history of thought that the attempt to understand it is well worth while, and its understanding throws light on some of the perplexing points in modern psychology.

Knowledge has in the past been described as being of two sorts. Sometimes the two sorts of knowledge have been designated as ''sensuous'' and ''intellectual,'' sometimes as ''perceptual'' and ''ideational.'' As a matter of fact these two divisions of the field of knowledge are not equivalent: The sensuous and the perceptual are not coextensive; neither are the intellectual and the ideational. Perhaps a better description of the two classes of knowledge is obtained by designating one as the *knowledge of sense perception* and the other as the *knowledge of inference or reason.* I perceive, on looking out of my window, that my barn is in flames: this is a form of knowledge I have of the event in progress. I know also, although my senses do not give me the direct information, nor do I strictly perceive it intellectually, that the barn was fired by lightning and that I will receive no insurance because my policy on the barn has expired. These things I know by inference or reason. The distinction between these two kinds of knowledge may not be as great as it seems to be, and further psychological analysis may show that it is valueless: but there can be no objection to the distinction as a preliminary or tentative one, and there can be no question but that the experiences classified in accordance with it really exist.

The psychologist holds that all knowledge may be included under the two headings above indicated. No knowledge which is neither perceptual nor inferential is taken account of by psychology. The mystic, on the other hand, holds that these two kinds of knowledge, or the totality of knowledge which may be tentatively classified under these two heads, do not exhaust the field. There is, the mystic insists, a *third kind of knowledge,* which, according to the mystical evaluation, ranks higher than either of the other two. Not necessarily higher in the sense of being more complex, or of being the result of a longer temporal course of development, but higher in value. This theory of a third kind of knowledge is the essential and fundamental point in mysticism.

Mystics and mysticism in the strict sense of the terms have existed in all civilized European countries for the last fourteen hundred years at least; yet in spite of this wide temporal and geographical distribution there is a remarkable simplicity and uniformity in the mystical declaration of principles wherever found. There are a number of conventional names, all of which are admitted to be metaphorical, for the act or fact of knowing in this assumed third way. Three terms in especial have been employed in various languages to designate this act. These are the terms *union, love,* and *ecstasy.* ''Union'' emphasizes what is claimed as the fundamental characteristic of this act, namely that the subject who knows, and the object which is known, become in the act one and the same, by the one being absorbed into the other.* ''Love'' is metaphorically significant because in its literal use it signifies the force which attracts and binds together two individuals. It was, in a more general sense, assumed by ancient Greek philosophy to be the force which binds together the different parts of the universe, making one out of many; just as in the more literal sense it is the force or attraction which binds two individuals, each incomplete in itself, together into a complete social individual capable of the total human functions. ''Ecstasy,'' which means literally a ''standing out,'' or getting out of, one's self, alludes to the

---

*''Mysticism is the art of union with reality. The mystic is a person who has attained that union in greater or less degree; or who aims at and believes in such attainment.'' Underhill: *Practical Mysticism,* p. 3.

same alleged fact: of the knowing subject losing its identity in the known object.

Since it is above intellect and above sense perception as these are conceived by psychology, the mystical third kind of knowledge cannot be communicated from one person to another, nor can it be described in language. Moreover, it cannot be thought by the mystic himself. The true mystic realizes this consequence of his hypothesis and admits his inability to think about, or to describe that which he knows in his ecstasy. He claims that all that is said about the mystic knowledge is mere metaphor; excepting only the statements that the knowledge may be obtained, and that its value is above all other values. Plotinus, for example, says:

It (unity) is unspeakable and undescribable. Nevertheless we speak of it, we write about it, but only to excite our souls by our discussions, and to direct them towards this divine spectacle, just as one might point out the road to somebody who desires to see some object. (*Enn.* VI, Bk. IV, 4.)

European mysticism is directly traceable in the line of historical descent from an early period of the Christian Era. Its connection with Oriental mysticism is problematic, in spite of the strong resemblances between the two. It is possible that the European mysticism owes something to the Oriental: it is also possible that the indebtedness is largely in the other direction. This problem is of little consequence for the understanding of European mysticism, whereas the tracing of the lineage in the West is important, since the theories and even the phraseology of the latter day mystics are essentially those of the earliest members of the school and are directly derived from them. In spite of changes in style, differences in the purposes of application, and variations in the expansion of details, the basic ideas have been little changed throughout.

The historical source of modern mysticism is the small collection of writings of a certain Dionysius,* who has been supposed to have been the Dionysius converted by Paul on the Areopagus or Mars Hill, and who is therefore called "Dionysius the Areopagite." He is identified with St. Denys or Denis, the Patron Saint of France and is supposed to have been the first Bishop of Athens. The more weighty critics doubt the authenticity of the writings in question and ascribe them to a date about 500 A.D., hence referring to their author as the "pseudo-Dionysius." Whatever may be the truth of this controversy the flood of modern mysticism was loosed from a Greek manuscript written by someone who called himself Dionysius.

The important writings of Dionysius were translated into Latin about 850 A.D. by Scotus Erigina,

---

*An English translation of Dionysius' writings has been made by Parker: *Dionysius the Areopagite,* 1897.

the organizer of the University of Paris. Thus not only by the teaching of Erigina and his pupils, but also by the dissemination of the Latin version of Dionysius' writings from the University of Paris, the course of modern philosophy, and in a still larger degree the course of religious speculation, has been seriously affected. The Medieval mysticism emanating from Paris was directly responsible for the later mystical schools which flourished in different parts of Europe at different periods. German mysticism, as represented by the three Dominican Monks—Meister Eckhardt (1260-1329 *circa*,) Tauler (*floruit* 1300-1316), Suso (1300-1365 *circa*), and the Theologica Germanica (written by a member of the "Friends of God" in the middle of the fourteenth century); and Flemish mysticism, represented by Ruysbroeck (1293-1381) together constitute the third great phase in the development of Western mysticism.

Spanish mysticism, represented by Juan de la Cruz (1542-1591) and Santa Teresa (1515-1582); the French mysticism of the Quietists represented by Madame Guyon (1648-1717); and the Anglo-American mysticism of Coleridge, Emerson, and Christian Science, while flowing from the historical sources in an easily traceable current are confused and mingled with much quasi-mysticism and pseudo-mysticism. The Neo-Flemish mysticism of Maeterlinck on the other hand, is a crystal pure

stream from undefiled ancient sources. In Maeterlinck is set forth the spirit of Dionysius and of the
other great mystics in such fashion as to make
Maeterlinck one of the company which his psychological adversaries must admire.

At the present day pure mysticism is increasing
in its spread and influence along with a dark and
muddy current of quasi-mysticism and pseudo-
mysticism. The perpetual conflict between science
and mysticism was never more acute than at the
present day, and it is because of the vital nature
of this conflict that it behooves us to examine carefully the foundations of true mysticism in order
that we may recognize it and its bastard progeny
however they may be disguised.

The principles and expressions of the mysticism
of Dionysius the Areopagite agree closely with
those of the so-called Alexandrian philosophy: so-
called because of its dissemination from the city of
Alexandria in Egypt. The first philosopher of this
school of whom we have definite knowledge was
Ammonius Saccas, who taught in Alexandria between 170 and 243 A.D. He was the son of Christian parents but abandoned Christianity for philosophy. The most important member of the school
was Plotinus (205-270 *circa*), a Greek,. born in
Lycopolis in Egypt; who studied under Ammonius in Alexandria for eleven years, went to
Rome about 244, and there taught philosophy until

his death in 270. The theories of Plotinus were edited by his pupil Porphyry in six *Enneads* or divisions of nine books each. Porphyry, who was an anti-Christian, also wrote a biography of Plotinus from which our information concerning that philosopher is in the main derived.

Plotinus considered himself a follower of Plato's philosophy and as the reestablisher of pure Platonism. The resemblance to the Plato of the *Banquet* and *Phoedrus* is clearly recognizable, and the Alexandrian philosophy is usually called neo-Platonism. Nevertheless, Semitic influences are discernible in this philosophy, although the sources are obscure. Plotinus was evidently familiar with the writings of Philo Judeaus, (20 B.C.—40 A.D.) the Jewish philosopher of Alexandria; but Porphyry denies that his master was influenced by Philo.

Parker and others think that the Alexandrian philosophy was derived from the writings of Dionysius. It is, however, more probable that Dionysius obtained his views from the Alexandrians. Certainly there is such marked resemblance between them that historical connection is hardly to be doubted.

According to the Alexandrians, that which is known, in the higher or third kind of knowledge is Divine Being or God. In the act of knowing, therefore—in union or ecstasy—the knower is absorbed into and is indistinguishable from the Divine

Known. This union is not attained at any moment at which the mystic may desire it, but is the consummation of long effort and achieved but occasionally. Plotinus, according to Porphyry, attained the mystic experience but four times during his life time and Porphyry himself achieved it only once.

That is how this divine man, who by his thoughts often aspired to the first (principle), to the divinity superior (to intelligence), climbing the degrees indicated by Plato (in his Banquet), he held the vision of the formless divinity, which is not merely an idea, being founded on intelligence and the whole intelligible world. I, myself, had the blessed privilege of approaching this divinity, uniting myself to him, when I was about sixty-eight years of age.

That is how "the goal seemed to him located near him." Indeed, his goal, his purpose, his end was to approach the supreme divinity, and to unite himself with the divinity. While I dwelt with him, he had four times the bliss of reaching that goal, not merely potentially, but by a real and unspeakable experience. Porphyry, Life of Plotinus, XXIII: Guthrie, *Plotinus' Complete Works*, Vol. I, pp. 33-34.

There are two terms used by Dionysius which are of exceptional interest because these or their equivalents are found in the writings of the Alexandrian school and of the later mystics. One of these terms is *Agnosia* which means literally "lack of knowledge." The other is *Divine Gloom*. Both of these are used to describe the mystic knowledge and the mystic object. According to the mystic theory, the third kind of knowledge is so far above ordinary cognition that it may be described as no knowledge at all: while it is analogous to knowledge, it so far transcends psychological limitations that the difference is more important than the likeness. Hence "Agnosia" is held to be more descriptive than is "knowledge," and "darkness" the more accurate symbol than "light." This paradoxical method of description is a deliberate indication of the claim that, strictly speaking, the experience is indescribable. Thus Dionysius:

Darkness becomes invisible by light, and especially by much light. Varied knowledge, and especially much varied knowledge, makes the *Agnosia* to vanish. Take this in a superlative, but not in a defective sense, and reply with superlative truth, that the *Agnosia*, respecting God, escapes those who possess existing light, and knowledge of things being; and his pre-eminent darkness is both concealed by every light, and is hidden from every knowledge. And, if anyone, having seen God, understood what he saw, he did not see *Him*, but some of His creatures that are existing and known. But He himself, highly established above mind, and above essence, by the very fact of His being wholly unknown, and not being, both is superessentially, and is known above mind. And the all-perfect *Agnosia*, in its superior sense, is a knowledge of Him, Who is above all known things. Dionysius, Letter to Gaius Therapeutes: Parker, Part I, p. 141.

We pray to enter within the super-bright gloom, and through not seeing and not knowing, to see and to know that the not to see nor to know is itself the above sight and knowledge. For this is veritably to see and to know and to celebrate superessentially the Superessential, through the abstraction of all existing things, just as those who make a life-like statue, by extracting all the encumbrances which have been placed upon the clear view of the concealed, and by bringing to light, by the mere cutting away, the genuine beauty concealed in it. And, it is necessary, as I think, to celebrate the abstractions in an opposite way to the definitions. For, we used to place these latter by beginning from the foremost and descending through the middle to the lowest, but, in this case, by making the ascents from the lowest to the highest, we abstract everything, in order that, without veil, we may know that *Agnosia*, which is enshrouded under all the known, in all things that be, and may see that superessential gloom, which is hidden by all the light in existing things. Dionysius: Mystic Theology, Caput II, sec. I. Parker, Part I, p. 133.

Thus also Plotinus:

The principal cause of our uncertainty is that our comprehension of the One comes to us neither by scientific knowledge, nor by thought, as the knowledge of other intelligible things, but by a presence which is superior to science. When the soul acquires the scientific knowledge of something, she withdraws from unity and ceases being entirely one; for science implies discursive reason and discursive reason implies manifoldness. (To attain Unity) we must therefore rise above science, and never withdraw from what is essentially One; we must therefore renounce science, the objects of science, and every other right (except that of the One); even to that of beauty; for beauty is posterior to unity, and is derived therefrom, as the day-light comes from the sun. That is why Plato says of (Unity) that it is unspeakable and undescribable. Nevertheless we speak of it, we write about it, but only to excite our souls by our discussions, and to direct them towards this divine spectacle, just as one might point out the road to somebody who desires to see some object. Instruction, indeed, goes - as far as showing the road, and guiding us in the way; but to obtain the vision (of the divinity), is the work suitable to him who has desired to obtain it.

If your soul does not succeed in enjoying this spectacle, if she does not have the intuition of the divine light, if she remains cold and does not, within herself, feel a rapture such as that of a lover who sees the beloved object, and who rests within it, a rapture felt by him who has seen the true light, and whose soul has been overwhelmed with brilliance on approaching this light, then you have tried to rise to the divinity without having freed yourself from the hindrances which arrest your progress, and hinder your contemplation. You did not rise alone, and you retained within yourself something that separated you from Him; or rather, you were not yet unified. Though He be absent from all beings, He is absent from none, so that He is present without being present. Plotinus: Enn. VI, Bk. IV, 4. Guthrie: *Plotinus' Complete Works*, Vol. I, pp. 154-155. Taylor: *Select Works of Plotinus*, pp. 306-307.

For, in order to express something, discursive reason is obliged to go from one thing to another, and successively to run through every element of its object. Now what can be successively scrutinized in that which is absolutely simple? It is, therefore, sufficient to reach Him by a sort of intellectual contact. Now at the moment of touching the One, we should neither be able to say anything about Him, nor have the leisure to speak of Him: Only later is it possible to argue about Him * * * The true purpose of the soul is to be in contact with this light, to see this light in the radiance of this light itself, without the assistance of any foreign light, to see this principle by the help of which she sees. Indeed, it is the principle by which she is enlightened that she must contemplate as she gazes at the sun only through its own light. Now how shall we succeed in this? By cutting off everything else. Plotinus, Enn. V, Bk. III, 17. Guthrie: *Plotinus' Complete Works*, Vol. IV., pp. 1120-21. Taylor: *Select Works of Plotinus*, p. 288.

It is characteristic of the Alexandrian mysticism and also characteristic of some of the later mysticisms that the good and the beautiful are identified. That which is the object of the mystic knowledge is the reality transcendent to the reality found in the world of psychological experience. This reality is good and also beautiful; thus epistemology, ethics and esthetics are identified, the three sciences becoming for the mystic, one and the same discipline. If we bear this in mind many of the terms used by the early and later mystics become significant. The identification of mystic knowledge with love has a multiple importance. It is directly derived from the early Greek philosophy in which Eros is the directing power which coordinates the diverse parts of the universe, supplying the "action at a distance" which is the necessary concept for naive physical speculation. On the other hand, the use and elaboration of the concept of love by the mystics may indicate a vague recognition of the erotic nature of "ecstasy." Plotinus' use of the term is typical.

Another proof that our welfare resides up there is the love that is innate in our souls, as is taught in the descriptions and myths which represent love as the husband of the soul. In fact, since the soul, which is different from the divinity proceeds from Him, she must necessarily love Him; but when she is on high her love is celestial; here below, her love is only commonplace; for it is on high that dwells the celestial Venus (Urania); while here below resides the vulgar adulterous Venus. Now every soul is a Venus, as is indicated by the myth of the birth of Venus and Cupid, who is supposed to be born simultaneously with her. So long as she remains faithful to her nature, the soul therefore loves the divinity, and desires to unite herself to Him, who seems like the noble father of a bride who has fallen in love with some handsome lover. When however the soul has descended into generation, deceived by the false promises of an adulterous lover, she has exchanged her divine love for a mortal one. Then, at a distance from a father, she yields to all kinds of excesses. Ultimately, however, she grows ashamed of these disorders; she purifies herself, she returns to her father, and finds true happiness with Him. How great her bliss then is can be conceived by such as have not tasted it only by comparing it somewhat to earthly love-unions, observing the joy felt by the lover in obtaining her whom he loves. But such mortal and deceptive love is directed only to phantoms; it soon disappears because the real object of our love is not these sense-presentations, which are not the good we are seeking. On high only is the real object of our love; the only one with which we could unite or identify ourselves, which we could intimately possess, because it is not separated from our soul by the covering of our flesh. This that I say will be acknowledged by any one who has experienced it; he will know that the soul then lives another life, that she advances towards the Divinity, that she reaches Him, possesses Him, and in his condition recognizes the presence of the Dispenser of the true life. Then she needs nothing more. On the contrary, she has to renounce everything else to fix herself in the Divinity, alone, to identify herself with Him, and to cut off all that surrounds Him. We must therefore hasten to issue from here below, detaching ourselves so far as possible from the body to which we still have the regret of being chained, making the effort to embrace the Divinity by our whole being, without leaving in us any part that is not in contact with Him. Then the soul can see the Divinity and herself, so far as is possible to her nature. She sees herself shining brilliantly, filled with intelligible light; or rather, she sees herself as a pure light, that is subtle and weightless. She becomes Divinity, or, rather she is divinity. In this condition the soul is a shining light. If later she falls back into the sense-world, she is plunged into darkness. Plotinus, Enn. VI, Bk. IX, 9. Guthrie: *Plotinus' Complete Works*, Vol. I, pp. 166-168. Taylor: *Select Works of Plotinus*, pp. 317-319.

The comparison of this passage with one from a modern mystic is not without interest:

And it is in this common fatherland also that we chose the women we loved, wherefore it is that we cannot have erred, nor can they have erred either. The kingdom of love is, before all else, the great kingdom of certitude, for it is within its bounds that the soul is possessed of the utmost leisure. There, truly, they have naught to do but to recognize each other, offer deepest admiration, and ask their questions—tearfully, like the maid who

has found the sister she had lost—while, far away from them, arm
links itself in arm and breaths are mingling. * * * At last
has a moment come when they can smile and live their own life—
for a truce has been called in the stern routine of daily existence—
and it is perhaps from the heights of this smile and these ineffable
glances that springs the mysterious perfume that pervades love's
dreariest moments, that preserves for ever the memory of the time
when the lips first met. * * *

It would seem that women are more largely swayed by destiny
than ourselves. They submit to its decrees with far more simplicity; nor is there sincerity in the resistance they offer. They
are still nearer to God, and yield themselves with less reserve to
the pure workings of the mystery. And therefore is it, doubtless,
that all the incidents in our life in which they take part seem to
bring us nearer to what might almost be the very fountainhead of
destiny. It is above all when by their side that moments come,
unexpectedly, when a ''clear presentiment'' flashes across us, a presentiment of a life that does not always seem parallel to the life
we know of. They lead us close to the gates of our being. May
it not be during one of those profound moments, when his head is
pillowed on a woman's breast, that the hero learns to know the
strength and steadfastness of his star? And indeed will any true
sentiment of the future ever come to the man who has not had his
resting place in a woman's heart? Maeterlinck, On Women: *The
Treasure of the Humble,* pp. 81-83.

The identity of the ''love''* of Maeterlinck with
the mystic knowledge is perhaps not evident in the
above, but is made so in the following:

THE SOUL'S HUNGER FOR GOD

Here there begins an eternal hunger, which shall nevermore be
satisfied. It is the yearning and the inward aspiration of our fac-

---

*It cannot be fairly said that the use of the term "love" as a name for
mystic knowledge is *entirely* metaphorical, in spite of the mystics' own statements. There seems to be for the mystic a certain identity in the sex relation in its romantic form, and the union with reality. For the scientific
psychologist, the suggestion of identity is most illuminating.

ulty of love, and of our created spirit towards an uncreated good. And as the spirit desires joy, and is invited and constrained by God to partake of it, it is always longing to realize joy. Behold then the beginning of an eternal aspiration and of eternal efforts, while our impotence is likewise eternal. These are the poorest of all men, for they are eager and greedy, and they can never be satisfied. Whatever they eat or drink, they can never have enough, for this hunger lasts continually. For a created vessel cannot contain an uncreated good, and hence that continual struggle of the hungry soul, and its feebleness which is swallowed up in God. There are here great banquets of food and drink, which none knoweth saving he who partakes of them; but full satisfaction of joy is the food which is ever lacking, and so the hunger is perpetually renewed. Yet streams of honey flow within reach, full of all delights, for the spirit tastes these pleasures in every imaginable way, but always according to its creaturely nature and below God, and that is why the hunger and the impatience are without end. Maeterlinck, Ruysbroeck and the Mystics: *Selected Passages,* p. 147.

For certain of the later mystics the object known in the mystic experience is not always God; it may be another human soul. For Maeterlinck the knowledge of other souls is of paramount importance, as the following quotations show:

I have said elsewhere that the souls of mankind seemed to be drawing nearer to each other, and even if this be not a statement that can be proved, it is none the less based upon deep-rooted, though obscure, convictions. It is indeed difficult to advance facts in its support, for facts are nothing but the laggards, the spies and camp followers of the great forces we cannot see. But surely there are moments when we seem to feel, more deeply than did our fathers before us, that we are not in the presence of ourselves alone. Neither those who believe in a God, nor those who disbelieve, are found to act in themselves as though they were sure of being alone. We are watched, we are under strictest supervision, and it comes from elsewhere than the indulgent darkness of each man's conscience. Perhaps the spiritual vases are less closely sealed now than in bygone days, perhaps more power has come to the waves of the sea within us? I know not: all that we can state with certainty is that we no longer attach the same importance to a certain number of traditional faults, but this is in itself a token of a spiritual victory. Maeterlinck, Mystic Morality: *The Treasure of the Humble*, p. 62.

A time will come, perhaps—and many things there are that herald its approach—a time will come perhaps when our souls will know of each other without the intermediary of the senses. Certain it is that there passes not a day but the soul adds to its ever-widening domain. It is very much nearer to our visible self, and takes a far greater part in all our actions, than was the case two or three centuries ago. A spiritual epoch is perhaps upon us; an epoch to which a certain number of analogies are found in history. For there are periods recorded, when the soul, in obedience to unknown laws, seemed to rise to the very surface of humanity, whence it gave clearest evidence of its existence and of its power. And this existence and this power reveal themselves in countless ways, diverse and unforeseen. It would seem, at moments such as these, as though humanity were on the point of struggling from beneath the crushing burden of matter that weighs it down. A spiritual influence is abroad that soothes and comforts; and the sternest, direst laws of Nature yield here and there. Men are nearer to themselves, nearer to their brothers; in the look of their eyes, in the love of their hearts, there is deeper earnestness and tenderer fellowship. Their understanding of women, children, animals, plants,—nay, of all things, becomes more pitiful and more profound. Maeterlinck, The Awakening of the Soul: *The Treasure of the Humble*, p. 25.

It is idle to think that, by means of words, any real communication can ever pass from one man to another. The lips or the tongue may represent the soul, even as a cipher or a number may represent a picture of Memling; but from the moment that we have *something to say to each other,* we are *compelled* to hold our peace; and if at such times we do not listen to the urgent commands of silence, invisible though they be, we shall have suffered an eternal loss that all the treasures of human wisdom cannot make good; for we shall have let slip the opportunity of listening to another soul and of giving existence, be it only for an instant, to our own; and many lives there are in which such opportunities do not present themselves twice. * * *

It is only when life is sluggish within us that we speak: only at moments when reality lies far away, and we *do not wish* to be conscious of our brethren. And no sooner do we speak than something warns us that the divine gates are closing. Thus it comes about that we hug silence to us, and are very misers of it; and even the most reckless will not squander it on the first comer. There is an instinct of the superhuman truths within us that warns us that it is dangerous to be silent with one whom we do not wish to know, or do not love; for words may pass between men, but let silence have had its instant of activity, and it will never efface itself; and indeed the true life, the only life that leaves a trace behind, is made up of silence alone. Bethink it well, in that silence to which you must again have recourse, so that it may explain itself, by itself; and if it be granted to you to descend for one moment into your soul, into the depths where the angels dwell, it is not the words spoken by the creature you loved so dearly that you will recall, or the gestures that he made, but it is, above all, the silences that you have lived together that will come back to you; for it is the *quality* of those silences that alone revealed the quality of your love and your souls. Maeterlinck, Silence: *The Treasure of the Humble*, p. 4.

No sooner are the lips still than the soul awakes, and sets forth on its labours; for silence is an element that is full of surprise, danger and happiness, and in these the soul possesses itself in freedom. If it be indeed your desire to give yourself over to another, be silent; and if you fear being silent with him—unless this fear be the proud uncertainty, or hunger, of the love that yearns for prodigies—fly from him, for your soul knows well how far it may go. There are men in whose presence the greatest of heroes would not dare to be silent; and even the soul that has nothing to conceal trembles lest another should discover its secret. Some there are that have no silence, and that kill the silence around them, and these are the only creatures that pass through life unperceived. To them it is not given to cross the zone of revelation, the great zone of the firm and faithful light. We cannot conceive what sort of man is he who has never been silent. It is to us as though his soul were featureless. ''We do not know each other yet,'' wrote to me one whom I hold dear above all others, ''we have not yet dared to be silent together.'' And it was true: already did we love each other so deeply that we shrank from the superhuman ordeal. And each time that silence fell upon us—the angel of the supreme truth, the messenger that brings to the heart the tidings of the unknown —each time did we feel that our souls were craving mercy on their knees, were begging for a few hours more of innocent falsehood, a few hours of ignorance, a few hours of childhood. * * * And none the less must its hour come. It is the sun of love, and it ripens the fruit of the soul, as the sun of heaven ripens the fruits of the earth. Maeterlinck, Silence: *The Treasure of the Humble,* p. 13.

In connection with Maeterlinck's pronounced erotism it is interesting to note that he elevates woman to a higher rank of mystical capacity than man:

With reverence must we draw near to them, be they lowly or arrogant, inattentive or lost in dreams, be they smiling still or plunged in tears; for they know the things that we do not know, and have a lamp that we have lost. Their abiding place is at the foot itself of the Inevitable, whose well worn paths are visible to them more clearly than to us. And thence it is that their strange intuitions have come to them, their gravity at which we wonder; and we feel that, even in their most trifling actions, they are conscious of being upheld by the strong, unerring hands of the gods. I said before that they drew us nearer to the gates of our being; verily might we believe, when we are with them, that that primeval gate is opening, amidst the bewildering whisper that doubtless waited on the birth of things, then when speech was yet hushed,

for fear lest command or forbidding should issue forth, unheard.
* * *

She will never cross the threshold of that gate; and she awaits us within, where are the fountain-heads. And when we come and knock from without, and she opens to our bidding, her hand will still keep hold of latch and key. She will look, for one instant, at the man who has been sent to her, and in that brief moment she has learned all that had to be learned, and the years to come have trembled to the end of time. * * * Who shall tell us of what consists the first look of love, ''that magic wand made of a ray of broken light,'' the ray that has issued forth from the eternal home of our being, that has transformed two souls, and given them twenty centuries of youth. The door may open again, or close; pay no heed, nor make further effort, for all is decided. She knows. She will no longer concern herself with the things you do, or say, or even think; and if she notices them, it will be but with a smile, and unconsciously will she fling from her all that does not help to confirm the certitudes of that first glance. And if you think you have deceived her, and that her impression is wrong, be sure that it is she who is right, and you yourself who are mistaken; for you are more truly that which you are in her eyes than that which in your soul you believe yourself to be, and this even though she may forever misinterpret the meaning of a gesture, a smile or a tear. * * * Maeterlinck, On Women: *The Treasure of the Humble,* p. 89.

It is necessary to distinguish between genuine mysticism and certain types of confused thought which are more properly called quasi-mysticism and pseudo-mysticism. There is a great deal of loose writing and discourse which makes use of the mystical terminology, but which does not involve definite mystical hypotheses. This is especially characteristic of sermons and popular religious writings. It is very frequently difficult to determine whether one who uses the familiar mystical phrases really understands their significance. To this indeterminate type of thought the term *quasi-mystical* should be applied.

Another, and at the present time very popular line of belief is pseudo-mystical; that is to say, although much confused with mysticism, it is not really mystical at all. The pseudo-mysticism includes telepathy, clairvoyance, and other supernatural methods of acquiring information or knowledge, but which have no essential conception of a transcendent *kind* of knowledge. However unnatural the means of acquiring this knowledge— whether by the "telepathy" which scientific psychology positively discredits, or from the "spirits" towards which psychology is blankly agnostic,— the knowledge when acquired is of the usual perceptual and ideational type. This distinction between the true mysticism and pseudo-mysticism is especially important in that the former ought not to be judged by the absurdities of some phases of the latter.

Pseudo-mysticism is older and wider than modern spiritualism, and includes all modes of revelation: there is nothing truly mystical in visions or voices, or in any other supernatural means of acquiring sensuous or intellectual knowledge, whether it be the revelation of John the Divine or of the Delphic oracle, or an African soothsayer.

Here again, it is important to distinguish true mysticism from the pseudo-mysticism, regardless of the respect or veneration in which either may be held.*

A classic example of the pseudo-mystic is Teresa, the chief of the so-called "Spanish mystics." Teresa saw visions and heard voices, and had definitely marked bodily experiences. By divine revelation of various sorts she acquired miscellaneous knowledge of an intellectual order. All this is pseudo-mystical: only to a small extent, apparently, is her divinely vouchsafed knowledge of a true mystical type.

I do not say that the soul sees and hears when the rapture is at the highest,—I mean by at the highest, when the faculties are lost, because profoundly united with God,—for then it neither sees, nor hears, nor perceives, as I believe; but, as I said of the previous prayer of union, this utter transformation of the soul in God continues only for an instant; while yet it continues no faculty of the soul is aware of it or knows what is passing there. Nor can it be understood while we are living on the earth—at least, God will not have us understand it, because we must be incapable of understanding it. I know it by experience. St. Teresa: *Life*, Chap. XX, 24. Lewis' Translation, p. 170.

I saw in his hand a long spear of gold, and at the iron's point there seemed to be a little fire. He appeared to me to be thrusting it at times into my heart, and to pierce my very entrails; when he drew it out, he seemed to draw them out also, and to leave

---

*The question as to the validity of the information acquired by revelation is not dependent on the question as to the nature of the revelation experience. As James pointed out (Varieties of Religious Experience), the truth of a given statement is not affected by its source, although in the absence of definite demonstration of the truth, the probable source of the information may establish a presumption.

me all on fire with a great love of God. The pain was so great that it made me moan; and yet so surpassing was the sweetness of this excessive pain that I could not wish to be rid of it. * * * The pain is not bodily, but spiritul; though the body has its share in it, even a large one. It is a caressing of sweet love which now takes place between the soul and God, that I pray God of his goodness to make him experience it who may think that I am lying. St. Teresa: *Life*, Chap. XXVIII, 17. Lewis' Translation, pp. 266-267.

On another occasion I was tortured for five hours with such terrible pains, such inward and outward sufferings, that it seemed to me as if I could not bear them. Those who were with me were frightened; they knew not what to do, and I could not help myself. I am in the habit when these pains and my bodily suffering are most unendurable, to make interior acts as well as I can, imploring our Lord if it be his will, to give me patience, and then to let me suffer on, even to the end of the world. So, when I found myself suffering so cruelly I relieved myself by making these acts and resolutions, in order that I might be able to endure the pain. It pleased the Lord to let me understand that it was the work of Satan: for I saw close beside me a most frightful little negro, gnashing his teeth in despair at losing what he attempted to seize. * * * Another time, and not long ago, the same thing happened to me, though it did not last so long, and I was alone at the moment. I asked for holy water; and they who come in after the devil had gone away,—they were two nuns, worthy of all credit, and would not tell a lie ffor anything,—perceived a most offensive smell, like that of brimstone. I smelt nothing myself, but the odor lasted long enough to become sensible to them. St. Teresa: *Life*, Chap. XXXI, 3, 5. Lewis' Translation, pp. 283-285.

One night I was so unwell that I thought I might be excused from making my prayer; so I took my rosary, that I might employ myself in vocal prayer, trying not to be recollected in my understanding, though outwardly I was recollected, being in my oratory. These little precautions are of no use when our Lord will have it otherwise. I remained there for a few moments thus, when I was rapt in spirit with such violence that I could make no resistance whatever. It seemed to me that I was taken up to heaven; and the first persons that I saw there were my father and my mother. I saw other things also; * * * St. Teresa: *Life,* Chap. XXXVIII, 1. Lewis' Translation, pp. 372-3.

Under the influence of anesthetics various individuals have obtained experience of a pseudo-mystical sort, sometimes verging on the genuinely mystical. In a rare essay from which James quotes in *The Will to Believe* (pp. 294-298), Benjamin P. Blood describes his experiences under anesthesia. Some of these are apparently ecstatic: in them Blood had perfect knowledge of the reality of things. He knew the universe so completely that there was no question that could be asked, but how he knew it he could not tell: when he came out from under the influence of the anesthetic he had merely the recollection of having possessed complete information.

A gentleman with whom I am acquainted who has been a great consumer of ether, having taken enormous quantities in short periods, has told me of several visits to heaven which he has made while under the influence. Many of the things he learned in heaven are of a pseudo-mystical sort, but at times he acquired divine illumination of perfect mystical knowledge. In usual cases, however, the experiences of a patient under anesthesia seem to to be pseudo-mystical and obviously emotional only.

In so far as we are able to examine and analyze the mystic experience second-hand from the reports of the mystics, we find certain characteristics which make it probable that the mystic experience is actually an intense emotional state: which indeed leave us little reason for supposing that the experience is anything other than emotional. On this account we have no reason for attempting to explain the mystic experience on other than common psychological grounds, and we have, therefore, no reason for doubting the facts of the experience and the good faith of the mystics in their attempts to describe it. In ecstasy or union—the noetic state which transcends all psychological cognition—the really cognitive elements are reduced well towards the zero point, leaving an emotional state which is almost purely affective and which is evidently exceedingly intense. The mystic's description of his own experience, far from being futile, is indeed highly significant. According to the mystic's claim the experience is transcendent; above intellect and above sense; in other words: purely emotional!

An individual who has had such an intense and almost purely emotional state will subsequently be able to recall the experience in a certain vague way. He will remember that he has been in such and such a condition; but since the emotion is not analyzed in the same definite way in which perceptual content may be, it will be remembered in a vague and sketchy manner. He will remember that he was in a blessed state: inevitably then he will ask himself, why this happiness? The average man supposes that happiness always has a reason for its occurrence. If he is happy, it is because there is something which gives him joy; and that which gives the supreme satisfaction is that for which he has been struggling longest and with the greatest effort. To a man whose ultimate goal is the acquisition of philosophic knowledge, but who has despaired of attaining that knowledge by ordinary lines of procedure, and who is in a condition of unhappiness and disappointment because of his failure, what is more natural than that in recalling the unusual and remarkable state of supreme satisfaction he should conclude that the joy was due to the attainment of that for which he had so long striven; since beyond that attainment he would ask no higher satisfaction? It is true that he cannot describe this illumination, he cannot even recall it: obviously then the knowledge was above description and above recollection.

In the mystical experience the sexual factor is evidently strong. I do not mean to say that the mystic recognizes the experience as explicitly sexual, and it usually is not sexual in the sense of being licentious or lewd, although in certain cases the lewd element is present. What I mean is, that in the experience there are certain factors which are conspicuously present in sexual emotion recognized as such, and which are probably due to physiological conditions of a distinctly sexual nature. It is not without significance that the description of ecstasy in many cases would pass equally well as a description of the sexual orgasm. Nor can it be a matter of chance that the state of union, of identification with the desired object, is insisted upon as the essential character of knowledge. Moreover, the ancient metaphor by which sexual intercourse is described as "knowledge" is an indication of the tendency to link sexual emotion with noetic experience.

The individualistic or anti-social aspect of mysticism is clearly marked. The mystic experiences and the considerations leading up to them are details which concern the individual and not the social group. The goal is an individual one, and progress towards it is the working out of an individual's salvation. Remove the conception that the sole spiritual consideration is one's own welfare, and the motive to mysticism vanishes. Even from the religious point of view, mysticism is a limitation which prevents the person from attaining the higher religious standpoint, which, crudely expressed, is that it is a matter of slight importance whether he is damned or not.

A universal characteristic of the mystic which

impels him to the mystic way, is a dissatisfaction with the scientific method and with scientific results. The mystic is essentially a tender-minded person who finds the hard labor and slow progression of science toward attainment of knowledge intolerably discouraging. Progress is so slow, and the goal so infinitely distant, that his soul "melts within him." It requires a high degree of hard-mindedness to be content with scientific progress, to bear the heavy weight of logic and intellectual clearness, and to be satisfied with the fact that the direction is right although the way is long.

The mystic moreover is not satisfied with the tentative nature of scientific truth, regardless of the tedium and the labor required to attain it. Science offers only working hypotheses of increasing exactness of application. It does not pretend to absolute or final certitude. The man who demands such certitude must obviously find some other way, and the mystic does demand a shorter and easier way. One quotation out of many similar passages illustrates the mystic's personal condition.

Mysticism is the pursuit of ultimate, objective truth, or it is nothing. "What the world calls mysticism," says Coventry Patmore, "is the science of ultimates, the science of self-evident reality." Not for one moment can it rest content with that neutrality or agnosticism with regard to the source and validity of its intuitions, which the psychologist, as such, is pledged to maintain. * * * The mystic is not interested in the states of his consciousness. He cares very little whether he is conscious or unconscious, in the body or out of the body. But he is supremely interested in knowing God, and, if possible, in seeing Him face to face. Inge, W. R.: *The Philosophy of Plotinus,* Vol. I, p. 3.

The tender-minded person longingly raises his eyes from the rough and tiresome road of science to look with despair toward the (to him) uninspiring goal, and soon ceases to struggle onward. In desperation he seeks some short cut, some route which will be free from the handicaps and difficulties through which science finds its way; and, finding a route which promises ease, he eagerly accepts it. Oppressed, discouraged, despairing of the simple and easy solution of the problem of human life; realizing that the attainment of scientific knowledge is laborious and slow to the point of impossibility; conscious of his inability to make and keep the exact logical distinctions which the imperious goddess of reason demands; the scientific straggler welcomes the glowing dream in which, by smothering the troublesome facts in the pleasant waters of illusion, he is in possession of the simple satisfaction which the hard taskmistress, Science, has denied him.

In freeing itself from the aims and methods of science, mysticism adopts without scruple a type of reasoning against which science constantly struggles: the type known to logicians as the fallacy of the *ambiguous middle term,* or as we might say, of the "sliding term." In scientific reasoning, it is important to use a term always in the same meaning: mysticism makes no such demands. A term is used to *suggest* the particular meaning desired and the same term is used to suggest different meanings in different places. "Cognition" or "knowledge" is used by the philosophical mystics sometimes in the real psychological meaning, sometimes to mean something quite different. Then, because the same term has been used in the two cases, the two meanings are treated (when it is convenient to do so) as if they were the same.

The ambiguous middle term is used by the mystic philosopher in an open and undisguised way. In mystical systems which are more disguised, the recognition of the fallacy is even more important and hence it will be treated more fully in a later place. It is the characteristic logical mark of mysticism, and wherever employed in a fundamental way, it marks as mystical the scheme in which it functions.

CHAPTER II

FREUD AND THE PSYCHOANALYSTS

One of the most important if not the most important mystical movement of the nineteenth century is currently known as *psychoanalysis* or psychanalysis. Starting with the work of Freud, a Vienna physician whose first definite publication in this line appeared in 1893, the school has developed until it now has important representatives in all European countries and in America, and has developed a "right wing" under the leadership of Jung of Zurich, and a "left wing" represented by Adler, in addition to the "central" tendency of Freud himself. Psychoanalysis began as a theory and technique in regard to the causes and treatment of the neurosis, but the theory has been extended until it takes in larger portions of the field of psychology and attempts to explain literature, art and religion and to supplant archæology.

The newly appointed head of the Department of Economics in a Western University expressed in my hearing the determination "to give Economics at last a real scientific (!) foundation in the psychopathology of Freud." Unfortunately death closed his career before this marvel could be accomplished. The greatest future development of the system is expected to be in the field of education, if the psychoanalysts have their way: at least they have been actively urging it upon teachers as the solution of educational problems.

A new science and application of pedagogy are being reared upon the data obtained by psychoanalysis, as witness the masterly work of Pfister recently published and made the forerunner of an important series of works on pedagogy under the leadership of Meumann and Messmer. Jeliffe: *The Technique of Psychoanalysis,* (1918) p. viii.

One may turn to "The Significance of Psychoanalysis for the Mental Science," by Otto Rank and Hans Sach (1913), translated by Charles R. Payne (1916), for full exposition of the application of Freudianism to literature, religion, ethnology, linguistics, philosophy, ethics, law, pedagogy and "characterology." So far, no one has expounded the psychoanalystic bases and interpretation for mathematics, physics and chemistry, but this may readily be accomplished.*

Appealing as it does to the mystical tendencies of human nature, dealing with the ever interesting topics of sex, and avoiding the deadly dullness of experimental science, psychoanalysis is especially captivating to those whose scientific training is

---

*The expected has happened. Since the above was written, Birdwood's *Sex Elements in the First Five Books of Euclid* has risen above the horizon. With such an excellent start, the exposition of the various sex perversions which the other mathematicians have expressed in their symbols and theorems will surely not be long delayed.

vague and whose methods of thinking are lacking in scientific precision. Moreover, being, to a large extent, an art as well as a theory, and producing "cures" of a striking nature in the field of mental medicine, it is becoming as strongly entrenched as its several rivals in the field and bids fair to be a formidable obstacle in the pathway of science for some years to come.

The essential postulate of psychoanalysis is the existence of something which is at one and the same time consciousness and not consciousness: sometimes designated as *the subsconscious* and sometimes as *the unconscious mind*. This concept, which can be traced back through Janet to Charcot under whom Freud studied in Paris, is almost the exact correspondent of the philosophical mystic's third kind of knowledge. It is knowledge in so far as an argument or explanation is to be based on its noetic character: it is not knowledge in so far as the argument requires the denial of that character. It differs from the mystic knowledge, however, in not being literally an experience but in being (in so far as it is conscious), conscious *stuff*. This characteristic of the subconscious is due to the dualistic foundation of the Anglo-German psychology from which psychoanalysis is germinated.

If we assume, as the older psychology based on Malebranche and Locke did assume, that there is a world of "mind" or "consciousness", easily distinguishable from a world of physical reality, but like it in that it is objective, we can understand the metaphysical basis of psychoanalysis. We must forget, therefore, for the moment, the present conception of scientific psychology according to which consciousness is merely a function of the total organism, and assume this old metaphysical theory for purposes of exposition.

Let us consider the mind as a house, having a dark basement and lighted superstructure. Things in the upper part of the house are "conscious" or "in consciousness;" things in the lower part of the house are "subconscious" or "in the subconscious mind." They are still in the house, as contrasted with things out of doors. This, or some other spatial analogy, must be constantly kept in view if we are to understand the way in which the doctrine of the subconscious is applied. In this house live ideas: ideas in the sense in which Malebranche and Locke used the term, distinct entities of an objective sort which, although they have origin and final dissolution, have yet a certain period of persistence during which they actually exist whether they are in the conscious part of the house or in the subconscious cellar. Whether one is aware of these ideas or not, they have much the same nature: moving them from the upper stories to the basement does not make them any the less mental, any the less ideas, although it may change them in some superficial and even in some important characteristics. In such a system, as in the older psychology, "awareness" (i. e., consciousness in the scientific psychological sense) is postulated in addition to the conscious stuff.*

The most important of the ideas or furniture of the mind are *desires,* which are instinctive productions of the human mind. These ideas can be dealt with by the mind or, to carry out our analogy, by some presiding authority in the house, in three ways. There may be action in accordance with them; or because of the conflict of these desires with other desires they may be relegated to a subordinate place and not acted upon; in which case apparently they die or are cast out harmlessly. Or in the third place the desire may be ignored: it may be thrust down into the dark cellar instead of being calmly assassinated on the ground floor. In this latter case the desire continues to live and retains its conative character. It is still a desire and possesses a certain energy in spite of the fact that the ruler of the house is no longer aware of it.

The thrusting of the desire out of consciousness into the subconsciousness, out of the upper story into the cellar, is called by the psychoanalysts *repression,* and a desire which has been thrust into

*This characteristic of the older metaphysics is clearly indicated by James: *Principles of Psychology,* I, p. 216. The distinction between awareness and consciousness as observable stuff is also drawn by Titchner: *American Journal of Psychology,* Volume 26, p. 265.

the subconscious cellar is a "repressed desire" or *complex*. Repression is, however, not done once for all. The repressed desire is perpetually striving to climb out of the cellar into the light and must be as perpetually held down, and it is this repression rather than the mere existence of the Kobold (complex) in the cellar which produces the neurosis.* From this schematism comes the conception of *conflict* between the desires and the inhibiting forces which thrust them into the cellar.

We have before us the picture of a strict gate-keeper who slams the door in the faces of uninvited guests. Since an affect which is present exercises not a momentary but a lasting activity, it is also not destroyed by a single repulse. Rather, there must be established a permanent frontier guard; that is, in other words a permanent interaction of forces, as a result of which, a certain psychic tension becomes inseparable from our mental life. That energy, the function of which is to protect consciousness from the invasion of the unconscious, we call, according as it appears in aggressive or defensive form, repression or resistance. Rank and Sachs: *The Significance of Psychoanalysis for the Mental Sciences,* p. 2. (Payne's Translation, 1916.)

The desires which are repressed are in general those which are normal to the individual (the owner of the mind-house) but are, in their particular manifestations, contrary to the conventions of society. The conflict which breeds neuroses,

---

*This is in accordance with the latest statements of Freud (*The History of the Psychoanalytic Movement*) but differs somewhat from Freud's earlier statement and from the point of view of other psychoanalysts. Thus Freud in his American lectures (*American Journal of Psychology,* Vol. 21, p. 194) likens the effects of repression to the ejection from a lecture hall of a rowdy who hangs about the door and creates more disturbance.

therefore, is the conflict between individual self-expression and social inhibitions. Theoretically, these repressed desires may cover a wide range, including theft, murder, and forms of self-expression which are considered by society boorishness rather than crime. Practically, however, repressed ideas are found by Freudians almost always to be sex desires. These desires are the grand group which society inhibits and discourages for its own purposes. "I am often asked" says Jung, " why it is just the erotic conflict rather than any other which is the cause of the neurosis. There is but one answer to this. No one asserts that this ought necessarily to be the case. But as a simple matter of fact it is always found to be so, notwithstanding all the cousins and aunts, godparents and teachers who rage against it." (*Analytic Psychology,* Long's Translation, p. 364.)

Normal sex desire as a whole may be repressed by individuals who have been taught to believe it low and wicked. This is one effect of certain social teachings which are represented by the doctrine that man is conceived in sin. The man or woman in whom this conviction has been developed shudders at his sex desires and strives to ignore them: whether they are thrust into the cellar or not the conflict is there. The sex desire as a whole is, however, not necessarily repressed. Desires outside the bounds established by law, by social convention, or by religious conviction may be repressed, although from the purely natural point of view these desires may be normal, that is to say, desires directed towards the opposite sex. Obviously, therefore, the man who leads an outwardly moral life is subject to grave dangers from the repression of desires which society considers polygamous or incestuous. The escape from these dangers is in either acting on the desires in defiance of law, convention and religion, or else the free admission to himself of the desires with rational refusal to act upon them. In no case must the desire be ignored: in no case must the individual assume or try to persuade himself that he really has not the lewd wish.

The repression of "normal" heterosexual desires, that is desires for normal intercourse with members of the opposite sex, is of least practical importance because it is the least apt to occur. More important is the repression of incestuous desire and still more important the repression of homosexual desire. This explains why libertines who admit apparently no social restraint upon their sex activities may yet be neurotic: may show the results of "repression." These individuals, as a matter of fact, are as apt to be neurotic as is the outwardly virtuous individual. That which the neurotic libertine represses is incestuous or homosexual desire, which according to the Freudians, is the most deadly of all. In addition to these, various specific perversions, such as masturbation, cunnilingus, sadism, exhibitionism, etc., may also be the subject of repressed desires. Some of these perversions may perhaps be considered as pathological, but masturbation, along with the general homosexual desire and two forms of incestuous desire (towards the mother and towards the father), which are generally supposed to be perversions, are considered by the Freudians as strictly normal and incident to every individual in some stage of development.

Sex desire is assumed by the Freudians to commence in the early weeks of infancy, as autoerotism: not merly as the autoerotism of Havelock Ellis (the originator of the term), but as actual desire. To use a technical psychoanalytic phrase, the *libido* (sex desire) of the child is fixed on himself. In a little later stage of development the libido becomes transferred to another person who may be either a person of the same sex or may be the parent of the opposite sex. Characteristically the child, before reaching puberty, goes through both of these stages, the incestuous, in which the boy's libido is fixed on his mother, the girl's on her father, and the homosexual, in which the libido is fixed in a more or less specific way on one or several members of the same sex.

This conception of sex development is obviously

possible only on the basis of the subconscious: the child obviously has no sex desire in the true meaning of the term although it may respond to sex stimulation.* Consequently (by psychoanalytic reasoning) the sex desire, not being conscious, must be unconscious or subconscious. Furthermore, the conception depends upon the assumption of a generalized sex desire or libido, not as an abstraction but as a definite force, in the same naive way in which the pre-Socratic philosophers conceived of Eros as a concrete force in the world.

The most troublesome complexes are those which originated in early life and of these, those which arise in late infancy or childhood are counted more deadly than those arising at puberty. Hence the term *infantilism* applied in a general way to the bases of neuroses. In practical analysis the central Freudian school tends to find the *Oedipus complex* and the *Electra complex* predominating, with homosexual complexes running a close third. By the term *Oedipus complex,* is indicated the sex desire of the boy towards his mother: by the *Electra complex* the result of the girl's repressing the fixa-

---

*The infantile evidence of sex-activity on which the Freudians depend are, in general, minor activities which are *later* incorporated in the general sex response. On this basis, absolutely all behavior may be said to be "sexual," and the word has merely been lost, a new term needing to be invented to cover what is ordinarily meant by the term "sexual." It must be borne in mind that for scientific psychology and common sense an activity is not necessarily sexual, as its first appearance, because later it assumes a sexual aspect. The panting, or labored breath of a child running away from a savage dog is not "sexual," although later sexual activities may involve not only labored breathing, but even running.

tion of her libido on her father, the terms being taken from the classic stories of Electra and Oedipus Rex.*

According to Freud, sexuality develops in the child in the first months of life. The normal sucking of the mother's breast is itself a sex activity which is extended through the sucking of the finger, the toe, or of an artificial nipple (pacifier). Afterwards the sucking is combined with manipulation of the breasts, genitals or other sexually sensitive parts of the body and so masturbation becomes the next step. Infants in whom autoerotic sucking is largely developed "as adults become passionately fond of kissing, tend to perverse kissing, or if men show a strong tendency to smoking or drinking" (Hitschmann). All children, according to the general psychoanalytic opinion, masturbate; all have pronounced sexual sensations from the anus in conjunction with normal defecation (anal eroticism). Incontinence of urine in children is psychoanalytically a substitute for sexual sensation, sex pleasure being at the bottom of it. Other manifestations said to occur in children are exhibitionism (delight

---

*The concept of the "mother complex" has a seeming application to cases of what are more ordinarily called "spoiled children" or "mother's darlings." These individuals who have been pampered in their childhood, and become even more troublesome to themselves and to others in adult life, miss the personal interest and sympathy, as well as the excessive protection extended by doting parents; and unless they find this personal support in a long-suffering wife, a priest, or a physician, they may become seriously neurotic. To this commonplace diagnosis psychoanalysis adds nothing but the fantastic notion of a repressed or unconscious sexual desire toward the mother, overlooking the obvious psychological mechanisms involved.

in being naked), the peeping tendency, and even Sadism and Masochism: the two latter being the active infliction of cruelty and the desire to suffer pain in connection with sex excitement.

Bjerre (*The History and Practice of Psychanalysis,* Barron's Translation, 1916, pp. 101, 102) points out that the Freudian theory of the Oedipus complex is taken from Luther, whose statement is in fact as scientific as that of any Freudian. Luther declared that the longing for woman arose because the individual begins in the life and body of the mother and is in fact in a very literal sense a part of the mother. Luther apparently does not attempt to explain the woman's longing for the man, although it might have been attributed to her origin in the male germ cell.*

Lay aside your doubts and let us evaluate the infantile sexuality of the earliest years. The sexual impulse of the child manifests itself as a very complex one, it permits of an analysis into many components, which spring from different sources. It is entirely disconnected with the function of reproduction which it is later to serve. It permits the child to gain different sorts of pleasure sensations, which we include, by the analogues and connections which they show, under the term sexual pleasures. The great source of infantile sexual pleasure is the auto-excitation of certain particularly sensitive parts of the body; besides the genitals are included, the rectum and the opening of the urinary canal, and also the skin and other sensory surfaces. Since in this first phase of child sexual life the satisfaction is found on the child's own body and has nothing to do with any other object, we call this phase after a

*See epitome theory in Jung: *Psychology of the Unconscious,* Hinkle's translation, p. 25.

word coined by Havelock Ellis, that of ''auto-erotism.'' The parts of the body significant in giving sexual pleasure we call ''erogenous zones.'' The thumb-sucking (*Ludeln*) or passionate sucking (*Wonnesaugen*) of very young children is a good example of such an auto-erotic satisfaction of an erogenous zone. Freud: Origin and Development of Psychoanalysis, *American Journal of Psychology*, Vol. 21, 1910, p. 209.

The child takes both parents, and especially one, as an object of his erotic wishes. Usually he follows in this the stimulus given by his parents, whose tenderness has very clearly the character of a sex manifestation, though inhibited so far as its goal is concerned. As a rule, the father prefers the daughter, the mother the son; the child reacts to this situation since, as son, he wishes himself in the place of his father, as daughter, in the place of the mother. The feeling awakened in these relations between parents and children, and, as a resultant of them, those among the children in relation to each other, are not only positively of a tender, but negatively of an inimical sort. The complex built up in this way is destined to quick repression, but it still exerts a great and lasting effect from the unconscious. We must express the opinion that this with its ramifications presents the *nuclear complex* of every neurosis, and so we are prepared to meet with it in a not less effectual way in the other fields of mental life. The myth of King Oedipus, who kills his father and wins his mother as a wife is only the slightly altered presentation of the infantile wish rejected later by the imposing barriers of incest. Freud: Origin and Development of Psychoanalysis, *American Journal of Psychology*, Vol. 21, 1910, p. 212.

* * * Hysterical patients suffer from ''reminiscences.'' At the bottom of every case of hysteria are found one or more events of premature sexual experience which belong to earliest youth; these may be reproduced in memory by persevering analytic work even after decades have intervened. At that time, these traumatic experiences were erroneously limited to neurotics; it soon became evident, however, that such experiences were often consciously remembered by individuals who remained perfectly healthy afterwards, hence the specific etiological agent in the causation of the neurotic symptoms could not lie in this circumstance. Hitschmann: *Freud's Theory of the Neurosis*, Payne's Translation, p. 11.

These studies can be made very precise. By them it can be shown that certain incidents of the sexual life conduce to such or such a pathological symptom. In fact, we can ascertain that the unfortunate sexual experience usually took place in infancy. "If the original sexual experience does not take place before the eighth year, hysteria will never follow as a consequence." The trace of the first sexual traumatism is, in the beginning, insignificant; later, toward the age of puberty, a conflict takes place between the sexual instinct and social ethics. This conflict causes a repression into the subconscious of the memory of various sexual scenes which the young man or woman has witnessed and the neurosis appears. This takes different forms according to the nature of the initial traumatism. If the child has taken a passive part in these sexual experiences—bear in mind this must occur before the eighth year—the neurosis later takes the form of hysteria. If, on the contrary, the child has been the aggressor, has taken the active part, the neurosis takes the form of obsessions and phobias, more properly psychasthenia. This would seem to be the reason that hysteria is more frequent in women and psychasthenia in men (?). In his study, Zur Aetiologie der Hystérie, 1896, Freud declared that these pathological discoveries would be to neuropathology what the discovery of the sources of the Nile had been to geography, that is to say, the greatest discovery in this science of the twentieth century. The other neuroses, moreover, have equally precise causes; masturbation is the only cause of neurasthenia; the anxiety neurosis (which Freud considers as a special disease) is caused by incomplete coitus or exaggerated abstinence, etc. These interpretations therefore, permit of a very precise diagnosis.

It is only just to say that later, in 1905, Freud realized that he has been mistaken on some points by the inexact memories of some patients, and he seemed no longer to give so precise an etiology to the various neuroses. To quote Ladame, Freud seemed to have relinquished the discovery of the sources of the Nile. But he always maintains the fundamental principle, namely, "that in the normal sexual life a neurosis is impossible." He continues

to give to the neuroses, and even to certain psychoses such as
dementia præcox, a single and truly specific cause, namely, a sexual
trouble caused by an experience which is conserved in the form of
a traumatic memory.

Of course the discovery of the specific causal agent of the neuroses gives a therapy at once simple and precise. Normal and
regular coitus will then suffice to cure all neuropathic disturbances.
Unfortunately, as Ladame remarks, this excellent medical prescription is not always easy to apply. Freud himself mournfully remarks that one great difficulty in following this advice is found
in the danger of the too frequent pregnancies which restricts normal and regular coitus. The precautions which are used to prevent conception, the unnatural practices, the using of various pre-
ventives, all of which are deplorable, are always injurious and
nullify the good effects of regular and normal coitus. Cruel
enigma! Freud begs physicians to devote all their efforts and intelligence to find a preventive that may satisfactorily meet all the
exigencies of coitus; something that can be used without danger
and without lessening enjoyment, and which will prevent both conception and injury to health. ''He who shall succeed in supplying
this lack in our medical technique will conserve the health and the
happiness of innumerable persons.'' Janet: Psychoanalysis, *Journal of Abnormal Psychology*, Vol. 9, 1914-15, p. 161.

Jung is more thoroughgoing than the central
Freudian school and pushes wherever possible the
complex back past infancy to the intrauterine life.
The desire (repressed) towards the mother is not,
strictly speaking, desire for sexual intercourse, or
at least it was not in its origin, although it may
have passed through that stage. Fundamentally,
it is the desire to return to the blissful condition
in utero in which one was protected by the mother
from all outside influences. The wing of the psychoanalytic movement which will carry the complex

back one stage more, and express it as the unconscious desire to return to the still more blissful stage of the unfertilized egg cell or the fertilizing sperm cell,* has not yet arisen; although this further development offers delightful possibilities in the way of schematic explanation of details which are lumped together in the Freudian and Jungerian theories, approaching even the artistic completeness of Plato's prefiguration of Freudianism in the Symposium.

The term "sex" is to a certain extent a term of sliding or variable meanings for the psychoanalyst. Certain ones explain that the term is not to be taken in its narrow significance as popularly used but indicates a much wider "biologic trend."

It is to this broad reproductive instinct, in all of its conscious and unconscious manifestations, that Freud has applied the term sexual. In this present volume on the Technique of Psychoanalysis, *sexual* means any human contact actual or symbolic by means of any sensory area with the object of the same or of the opposite sex, which has *productive creation* for its *purpose,* be it concretely in the form of a child, or symbolically as an invention, artistic production, or other type of mutual creative product. It does not apply to those contacts which have purely nutritive or self-preservation instinct behind it. And it does not apply solely to genital contacts. Jelliffe: The Oedipus Hypothesis. *The Technique of Psychoanalysis,* p. 52.

This is in defence against those who speak disparagingly of the Freudian system as reducing

---

*For the suggestion of this improvement I am indebted to Dr. Mildred W. Loring.

everything in life to a narrow and gross basis. Not much attention need be paid to this particular source of confusion, however, since Freud himself frankly disclaims any such flimsy *argumentum ad hominum* just as does Jung in the statement quoted above.*

The Freudian hypothesis of infantile sex life is founded on the specific fallacy known to the logicians as the fallacy of *secundum quid.* Reactions which later become a part of the general sex activity are found in the child, and therefore pointed out as evidence of sex activity. It is as if one should claim that the labored breathing produced by running to catch a street car is *sexual* because the same labored breathing may occur during certain stages of sex activity. As a matter of fact, there is no form of activity, and no form of instinct of the individual which is not at some time or other connected with the sex life, and the final consequence of the Freudian method is to define sex as *the whole universe,* which would leave us to hunt for a new term to use for what is meant by sex in science and common sense.

One term which the psychoanalysts have introduced is a somewhat valuable one for general pur-

*A similar camouflaging of the term "libido" occurs in some authors (Jelliffe, Chap. III) and is equally futile, since all of the terms of this group, when divested of their usual meanings, have no significance at all, and are useful to the Freudians only because the customary meaning is persistently present. This is a manifestation of the fallacy of ambiguous middle which will be pointed out later.

poses, although not strictly descriptive of the situation which it is intended to indicate. This is the term *wish-fulfillment* and refers to the tendency in human nature to get by an indirect route the fulfillment of those desires which it cannot obtain in a more normal manner, or at least to obtain in thought, satisfactions which cannot be obtained in actuality. The concept therefore is not actually of wish-fulfillment in the literal sense, but of wish-deception. This concept comes out most clearly in the phenomena of dreams, to the exposition of which we now turn. The great point historically at least in the technique of psychoanalysis is in the interpretation of dreams, and dream interpretation on a Freudian basis has attained an importance independent of its application to psychopathology.

The Kobold im Kellar—the complex—not only causes neuroses and certain other phenomena which we will mention later, but it is also the official cause of dreams. The dream, concisely speaking, is the attempt of the repressed desire to escape from the cellar into the half light of the upper story during the period of sleep. In the divided house of the mind there is a *censor* whose nature is not clearly indicated, but who is probably nothing more than the owner of the house. This censor keeps the cellar stairway during waking hours and prevents the demons from escaping upward. During the period of sleep the censor does not entirely cease his function but becomes somewhat uncritical and careless. Even so, the repressed desires cannot slip by him easily. The attempt to pass wakes him to the resumption of his function, unless the demon assumes a partial disguise of a character competent to avoid the censor's drowsy attention. Dreams, therefore, are the fantastic play of the desires which in their flimsy disguises have escaped from repression. As disguised, the desires are called *symbols,* that is to say, the central details of a dream symbolize or represent by analogy the repressed desires. Even on waking, the mind, or the censor in the mind, is usually unable to recognize the symbols in their true character and it requires the help of the expert psychoanalyst to identify the culprits.

I was once called upon to analyze the very short dream of a woman; she had wrung the neck of a little barking, white dog. She was very much amazed that she, ''who could not hurt a fly,'' could dream such a cruel dream; she did not remember having had one like it before. She admitted that she was very fond of cooking and that she had many times with her own hands killed chickens and doves. Then it occurred to her that she had wrung the neck of the little dog in her dream in exactly the same way that she was accustomed to do with the doves in order to cause the birds less pain. The thoughts and associations which followed had to do with pictures and stories of executions, and especially with the thought that the executioner, when he has fastened the cord about the neck of the criminal, arranges it so as to give the neck a twist, to hasten death. Asked against whom she felt strong enmity at the present time, she named a sister-in-law, and related at length her bad qualities and the malicious deeds with which she had

disturbed the family harmony, before so beautiful, after insinuat-
ing herself like a *tame dove* into the favor of her later husband.
Not long before there had taken place between her and the patient
a very violent scene, which ended by the patient showing the other
woman the door with the words: "Get out: I cannot endure a
biting dog in my house." Now it was clear whom the little white
dog represented, and whose neck she wrung in her dream. The
sister-in-law is also a small person, with an extraordinarily white
complexion. This little analysis enables one to observe the dream
in its displacing and so disguising activity.

Without doubt the dream has used the comparison with the biting dog, instead of the real object of the execution-fancy (the sister-in-law), smuggling in a little white dog, just as the angel in
the Biblical story gave Abraham a ram to slaughter at the last
instant, when he was preparing to sacrifice his son. In order to
accomplish this, the dream had to heap up memory images of the
killing of animals until by means of their condensed psychic energy the image of the hated person paled, and the scene of the
obvious dream was shifted to the animal kingdom. Memory images
of human executions serve as a connecting link for this displace-
ment. Ferenczi: The Psychological Analysis of Dreams, *American Journal of Psychology*, Vol. 21, 1910, p. 322.

It is too bad Ferenczi did not know of—or did not
think of— the popular superstition concerning the
erectile effect of hanging; and the resulting value
of a piece of the rope with which a man had been
hanged, as a charm for curing barrenness: this
would have worked into the interpretation admi-
rably.

Another patient dreamed of the corridor of the girls' boarding
school in which she was educated. She saw her own closet there
and desired to open it, but could not find the key, so that she was
forced to break the door. But as she violently opened the door, it
became evident that there was nothing within. The whole dream

proved to be a symbolic masturbation-phantasy, a memory from the time of puberty; the female genitals were, as so often happens, presented as a closet. But the supplement to the dream "there is nothing within" (*es ist nichts darin*) means in the Hungarian language the same as the German expression "it is no matter" (*es ist nichts daran*), and is a sort of exculpation or self-consolation of this sufferer from a bad conscience. Ferenczi: The Psychological Analysis of Dreams, *American Journal of Psychology*, Vol. 21, 1910, p. 324.

* * * Another, equally modest patient, told me this, which is an exhibition dream with somewhat altered circumstances: She was enveloped from top to toe in a white garment and bound to a pillar; around her stood foreign men, Turks or Arabs, who were haggling over her. The scene reminds one very strongly, apart from her enveloping garment, of an Oriental slave market; and indeed, analysis brought out that this lady, now so modest, when a young girl had read the tales of the "Thousand and One Nights" and had seen herself in fancy in many of the situations of the highly colored love scenes of the Orient. At this time she imagined that slaves were exposed for sale not clothed, but naked. At present she repudiates the idea of nudity so strongly even in dreams that the suppressed wishes which bear upon this theme can only come into being *when changed to their opposite*. Ferenczi: The Psychological Analysis of Dreams, *American Journal of Psychology*, Vol. 21, 1910, p. 315.

A patient, a woman aged 36, dreamt that she was standing in a crowd of school girls. One of them said: "Why do you wear such untidy skirts?" and turned up the patient's skirt to show how worn the underskirt was. During the analysis, three days after relating the dream, the patient for the first time recalled that the underskirt in the dream seemed to be a night-dress, and analysis of this led to the evocation of several painful memories in which lifting a nightdress played an important part; the two most significant of these had for many years been forgotten. Jones: Freud's Theory of Dreams, *American Journal of Psychology*, Vol. 21, 1910, p. 305.

She stood at the seashore watching a small boy, who seemed to be hers, wading into the water. This he did until the water covered him and she could only see his head bobbing up and down near the surface. The scene then changed into the crowded hall of an hotel. Her husband left her and she "entered into conversation with" a stranger. The second half of the dream revealed itself in the analysis as representing a flight from her husband and the entering into intimate relations with a third person, behind whom was plainly indicated Mr. X's brother, mentioned in the former dream. The first part of the dream was a fairly evident birth phantasy. In dreams, as in mythology, the delivering of a child *from* the uterine waters is commonly presented by distortion as the entry of the child *into* water; among many others, the births of Adonis, Osiris, Moses and Bacchus are well known illustrations of this. The bobbing up and down of the head in the water at once recalled to the patient the sensation of quickening she had experienced in her only pregnancy. Thinking of the boy going into the water induced a revery in which she saw herself taking him out of the water, carrying him to a nursery, washing him and dressing him, and installing him in her household.

The second half of the dream therefore represented· thoughts concerning the elopement, that belonged to the first half of the underlying latent content; the first half of the dream corresponded with the second half of the latent content, the birth phantasy. Besides this inversion in order, further inversion took place in each half of the dream. In the first half the child *entered* the water, and then his head bobbed; in the underlying dream thoughts first the quickening occurred, and then the child *left* the water (a double inversion.) In the second half her husband left her; in the dream thoughts she left her husband. Jones: Freud's Theory of Dreams, *American Journal of Psychology,* Vol. 21, 1910, p. 296.

A patient, a woman of thirty-seven, dreamt that she was sitting in a grandstand as though to watch some spectacle. A military band approached playing a gay martial air. It was at the head of a funeral which seemed to be of a Mr. X; the casket rested on a draped gun-carriage. She had a lively feeling of astonishment at the absurdity of making such an ado about the death of such an insignificant person. Behind followed the dead man's brother and one of his sisters, and behind them his two other sisters; they were incongruously dressed in a bright grey check. The brother advanced "like a savage" dancing and waving his arms; on his back was a yucca tree with a number of young blossoms. This dream is a good example of the second of the three types mentioned above, being perfectly clear and yet apparently impossible to fit into the patient's waking mental life. The true meaning of it, however, became only too clear on analysis. The figure of Mr. X veiled that of her husband. Both men had promised much when they were young, but the hopes their friends had built on them had not been fulfilled; the one had ruined his health and career by his addiction to morphia, and the other by his addiction to alcohol. Under the greatest stress of emotion the patient related that her husband's alcoholic habits had completely alienated her wifely feeling for him, and that in his drunken moments he even inspired her with an intense physical loathing. In the dream her repressed wish that he might die was realized by picturing the funeral of a third person whose career resembled that of her husband's and who like her husband, had one brother and three sisters. Further than this, her almost savage contempt for her husband, which arose from his lack of ambition and other more intimate circumstances, came to expression in the dream by her reflecting how absurd it was that anyone would make an ado over the death of such a nonentity, and by the gaiety shown at his funeral not only by all the world (the gay air of the band; her husband is, by the way, an officer in the volunteers, while Mr. X has no connection with the army), but even by his nearest relative (the brother's dancing, the bright clothes). It is noteworthy that no wife appeared in the dream, though Mr. X is married, a fact that illustrates the frequent projection on to others of sentiments that the subject himself experiences but repudiates.

In real life Mr. X, who is still alive, is an indifferent acquaintance, but his brother had been engaged to be married to the patient, and they were deeply attached to each other. Her parents, however, manoeuvered to bring about a misunderstanding between the two, and at their instigation, in a fit of pique, she married her present husband, to her enduring regret. Mr. X's brother was furiously jealous at this, and the pean of joy he realized in the dream does not appear so incongruous when we relate it to the idea of the death of the patient's husband as it does in reference to his own brother's death. His exuberant movements and "dancing like a savage" reminded the patient of native ceremonies she had seen, particularly marriage ceremonies. The yucca tree (a sturdy shrub indigenous to the Western States) proved to be a phallic symbol, and the young blossoms represented offspring. The patient bitterly regrets never having had any children, a circumstance she ascribes to her husband's vices. In the dream, therefore, her husband dies unregretted by anyone, she marries her lover and has many children. Jones: Freud's Theory of Dreams, *American Journal of Psychology*, Vol. 21, 1910, p. 292.

There isn't the minutest exaggeration here. Let me cite a few instances from articles I happen to have before me: "To those acquainted with the language of hysteria, such things frequently mean the opposite." (N. Y. Med. Jour., April 23, 1910.) "For those familiar with dream symbolism, her dreaming that the man put his hand in her pocket requires no analysis. The pocket is a frequent dream-symbol for the vagina." In this analysis the girl (whose dream was being interpreted) yearned for her brother "to put *his* hand in *her* pocket." The brother was, however, so to speak, only second fiddle, for she had craved for the hand of her own father to give her this delight, but he dying, by a transfer of *libido*, the desire fell upon the son, her brother, who was nearest like her father, etc. (Journal of Abnormal Psychology, Aug.-Sept., 1911, p. 194-5.) For "left" side being the "illegitimate"—always in connection with coitus or similar ecstasy, see Med. Record, Dec. 24, 1910. In one of the most *ardent* dream interpretations (N. Y., Med. Jour., June 14, 1913, p. 1234)—a young man (in the dream) raises a round white wooded basket to a girl. The contents were small seeds and white syrup. When the seeds were pressed they produced milky syrup, etc. Now this is the way this Freudian interprets it: "The basket she associated with the vagina, the seeds with chicken ovaries; and the fluid from the seeds meant to her milk from the breast and semen. The man in the dream says,

'here sip.' This meant to her intercourse. In her early childhood she used to play with small girls and they would suck each
other's clitores. This dream expressed the wish for cunnilingus with
her father, the idea of which she had cherished all her life.'' This
might be taken as the high-water mark of sexuo-analytic accom-
plishment. A half dozen lines further on this writer, who has just
given so remarkable an interpretation, says, ''It cannot be too
strongly emphasized that Freud's conception of the word sexual
does not limit itself to the *gross* sexual (the italics are not mine),
but embraces a wide scope of psychic manifestations of the sexual
life,'' and this after so abhorrent an ''interpretation'' as the
above. If you look through a dozen articles of these dream seers
you will find each one, in spite of his lullabying about Freud's
meaning of sexual, making out his patient to desire ''cunnilingus''
from her father, or as wishing to perform fellatio on him, or having her pockets picked, etc. You get the opinion that almost all
daughters desire this. (What an orgy such an ''evening'' at the
Psychoanalytic Society must be with all these brethren munching
their themes!) Haberman: A Criticism of Psychoanalysis, *Journal of Abnormal Psychology*, Vol. 9, 1914-15, p. 269.

The details of the uninterpreted dream are the
manifest content which make in many cases a deceptive drama apparently meaning something
entirely different from the hidden content which
the psychoanalyst finds through the consideration
of the details of the manifest content as symbols.
Primarily, symbols as illustrated in the above detailed dreams are strictly analogical, although by
an extension of the field of symbolization, the analogies may become somewhat stretched. Any vessel, bag, box, room, corridor or enclosure of any
sort represents the vagina or uterus. A stick, club
or weapon of any sort represents the phallus. A

forest, underbrush, or green field represents the pubic hair. A hill represents the mons veneris. Columns or pillars may represent the phallus or the thighs as the case may be. Attempting to accomplish something without success, as in attempting to run when the limbs seem paralyzed, represents sexual impotence. Nakedness is exhibitionism. An attack or fighting always represents coitus. So also eating, drinking, flying, going upstairs or up a hill or going into an enclosure or between objects. Sometimes the analogy is reversed; thus going downstairs or downhill may symbolize the ascent of the mons veneris since it is the reversal, (a simple trick of the complex to fool the censor), of the direct analogy.*

Thus the patient's own body is most frequently spoken of as a house. Nakedness of the body is frequently indicated by clothing, uniforms, draperies, hangings, nets, etc. Parts that show through are peeping and exhibitionism symbolisms. The male body is symbolized by flat things, the female body by irregular ones, mounds,

---

*The following list of symbols is drawn from Freud himself. Emperor and Empress (King and Queen) usually stand for the parents of the dreamer. Prince or princess for the dreamer himself. All long objects, such as canes, limbs of trees, snakes, umbrellas (because when put up they resemble an erection,) indicate the phallus. A frequent, not readily understood, symbol is the nail file (because of the rubbing and scraping?). Small boxes, band-boxes, caskets, closets, ovens, wagons, etc., correspond to the female body. Rooms in dreams are mostly ladies' rooms. The representations of entrances and exits will not be misunderstood, in this connection. The dream of going through a series of rooms is a brothel or harem dream. Tables, tables that are set, and boards are likewise women probably because of contrast. Since board and bed make the marriage, in dreams the first is often placed for the last, and so far as it applies, the sexual idea-complex is transported to the eating place. All complicated machines and apparatus in dreams are in great probability genitals, in the ascribing of which dream symbolism shows itself as untiring as wit may. Landscapes often signify female genitals. The locality "in which one was once before" may symbolize the mother's genitals. Children in dreams often signify the genitals, as men and women are occasionally disposed to call their genitals their "little one."

hills, rolling landscapes, etc. Climbing on flat surfaces, or balconies, indicate these differences.

The sexual act is largely symbolized by those types of movement which contain alternations of parts of the body or rapid backward and forward movements. Thus running, up or down stairs, dancing, swinging the arms, artificial respiration, movements, playing the piano, swinging in a swing, or hobby-horse, or ticking of a clock, metronome striking, etc. Much will depend upon the relations of the parts in the dream whether this symbolism is a true coitus wish or only a masturbatory wish. Thus five-finger exercises on the piano is frequently a purely masturbatory wish. Not infrequently the coitus is represented as a masturbatory type of coitus. For it should be remembered that such coitus has a masturbatory character. Thus a coitus as expressed as going up a pair of stairs usually has a more ethical significance than one going down a flight of stairs. The figure 3 is frequently used as a coitus symbol. It is used for other purposes as well. Thus one patient—a mild schizophrenic—states consciously she goes up three steps and stops, then three steps and stops, for if she does not she will not have a movement of the bowels. She is stating in a symbolic way—''with coitus she can have a baby''—the movement of the bowels referring to an infantile fecal birth phantasy.

The male organ is frequently symbolized as something long and thin—a dagger, umbrella, stick, cane, tree trunk, pillar, barrel, revolver, arrow, asparagus, banana, pear, corn cob, reptiles, fish, snakes, etc., etc., drain pipes, leaders, sprinkling pots, coffee pots, etc., often symbolize the male organ; the female genitals as muff, bag, box, chest, purse, pocket, chair, bed, hole, cave, church, crack, center of target, windows, doors, small rooms, cellar. The figure 2 is a frequent female symbolization. Hairy animals may be either organ as determined by the size and character. Fear of touching a dead bird in one patient was a definite masturbatory symbol. Playing with kittens another. Castration and masturbatory phantasies (fellatio and cunnilingus) are frequently associated with losing a tooth.

Potency and impotency symbols are frequently represented by flying machines, Zeppelins, balloons, trees, standing or falling, pillars standing or falling (Sampson). Flying is a frequent erection wish. Losing trains, or boats or busses or things—these are frequent impotency symbols.

Birth symbolisms center about water; going in or coming out; saving people, animals, objects from the water.

Death wishes are represented by reduction of the libido, going into the dark, going away, on journeys, on the railroad, boats, etc.

These are but a few of the more standard symbolizations, more precise details concerning which must be sought for in the works mentioned. Jelliffe: *The Technique of Psychoanalysis*, p. 141.

As is readily seen, anything that can be dreamed of has a ready sex interpretation. So that the telling of one's dreams to anyone versed in the gentle art of psychoanalysis is a matter in which your feelings of delicacy or prudence will dictate if you realize the possibilities. This is, however, not a matter of any vital consequence, since if the Freudians are right, we are all full of these sex repressions and hence none of us may be ashamed to look the rest of the world in the face; and if the Freudians be not right the whole matter is nothing more than a joke, although a smutty one.

Although dream symbolization commences in naive analogy, the psychoanalyst is not limited to such. The more clever of the dream demons, especially when harried by an unusually astute censor may assume disguises of more complex or unanalogical character. Jung explains that:

One loses oneself in one cul de sac after another by saying that this is the symbol substituted for the mother and that for the penis. In this realm there is no fixed significance of things. The only reality here is the libido for which ''all that is perishable is merely a symbol.'' It is not the physical actual mother, but the libido of the son, the object of which was once the mother. We take mythological symbols much too concretely and wonder at every step about the endless contradictions. These contradictions arise because we constantly forget that in the realm of fantasy ''feeling is all.'' Whenever we read, therefore, ''his mother was a wicked sorcerer,'' the translation is as follows: The son is in love with her, namely, he is unable to detach his libido from the mother-image. He, therefore, suffers from incestuous resistance. *The Psychology of the Unconscious*, Hinkle's translation, p. 249.

In any case the symbolism is not unambiguous. Even if we use analogy a given symbol may have analogies of several different sorts. No psychoanalyst, therefore, would give a final interpretation without the study of a number of dreams in which to compare the symbolism, and usually he will compare these with verbal association obtained by suggesting to the patient words and situations represented in the dreams. The method of ''association diagnosis'' is an important topic in itself and need not enter into the discussion. In many cases, however, the symbolism of a single dream is so coherent that the psychoanalyst will give a tentative interpretation requiring little modification from other dreams or from association. The technique of interpretation is easily acquired and interpretations which any clever person will make after a little practice are apt to satisfy the psychoanalyst. Some hitherto unpublished dreams which have been reported to me by various persons may be interesting in this connection. Some of them are so obvious that the reader may easily supply the Freudian interpretation.

I met A. B. and we proceeded to the shore of a very muddy stream. A. started to cross a bridge and I followed him after a short interval. After a time I lost sight of A. and gave my entire attention to the bridge, which stretched out from me in little hillocks. After a time I came to a place on the bridge which was lapped by the muddy water and seemed very insecure. As I made my way along this place I was forced to balance myself, keeping my legs spread far apart. I was very much frightened. I looked up and saw A. safe on the other shore.

This is a dream of a young man thoroughly familiar with Freudian methods, and contemplating matrimony. A. is a young groom, having been married about four months before, and is a close friend of the dreamer.

I and my mother and my father were on a Sparrow's Point car. Father got off at the car barn and mother and I stayed on until the car crossed the bridge, whereupon we got off. We intended to return for father.

The dreamer's mother is dead and his father lives on the Eastern Shore. By association I obtained the following data: preferred his mother to his father, greater intimacy and sympathy with mother. Had had some trouble with his father, and not on the best of terms with him now. Evidently ''mother complex.'' The wish (repressed) that father could have died instead of mother prominent in causation of dream.

I was in a room with some other men. We were bombarded from outside, knives being thrown through the windows of the room. I crouched down behind my desk (the room was a University class room) and held a book in front of my face. The knives struck all around but I was not hit.

The day before the dreamer, a scrupulous young man preparing for the ministry, had heard Prof. L. lecture on John Brown, describing an incident in which Brown and his men went to the door of a cabin, called the occupant out on some pretext, and then ran him through with their long knives. From association the book was clearly the Bible. The only attack suggested was an attack on principles, such as might be made by Freudian theories, on which he had recently heard me lecture. Psychoanalytically, the dream symbolizes the attack or menace of Freudian views on the moral and religious principles of the patient. He stated that the discussion of Freudianism had brought up in memory some of his earlier temptations in school.

I was riding on the back of a cow and the cow turned and stuck me with her horn. (Dream of a young lady.)

She is very fond of cows, using the expression, "I love cows; aren't they sweet? They have beautiful eyes." With regard to being stuck with the horn she was rather vague and when questioned as to how the cow had managed to stick her she said that the cow must have pushed her head straight back and struck her with both horns. When her attention was called to the fact that cows cannot make such movements, she said that a horse might have done this.

I was going from South Baltimore up town in a direction which I realized was parallel to my home and I went through a narrow alley beside the penitentiary. In some way I felt that I could see over the walls of the penitentiary and noticed some large scattered brown buildings, which I thought were somewhat like the buildings at Homewood. I walked through the alley very cautiously, fearing that I might be shadowed as a German spy. Passing a short distance beyond the penitentiary I came to a small chicken coop in a back yard. In the coop were two chickens, one being of a very beautiful brown color, and the other black and white, like a checker board. The spotted chicken was high up on a perch in the coop and a cat on the floor was evidently stalking her. I noticed that it was very easy for the cat to strike the brown chicken, but this did not occur. I picked up a small stone and hurled it at the cat, which then turned and followed me a short distance. I was afraid of being bitten on the right ankle and hurried away.

Starting from my knowledge that the dreamer's fiancée was named *White*, I determined to connect this dream with a flirtation with some other woman. By following up associations I was able to make him identify the "chicken" and the "cat."

One objection which might superficially be made to the interpretation of dreams *a la* Freud would be that the relater of the dreams may be lying, or may suffer from defective memory; in other words the dream as related may not be a true dream, but a fictitious construction. This however is actually not a serious objection, since the Freudians insist that the mechanism in the fabrication of a dream and in the fabrication of any other story are essentially the same. When a person deliberately constructs a fantasy, that which he will construct is determined by his complexes in the same way as that in which they produce a dream. This principle as we shall see later has far reaching application to all work of the constructive imagination, literary or scientific.

The following artificial dream constructed by one of my students illustrates this point sufficiently well.

I am alone, slowly climbing a gently sloping hill, on the top of which appears a group of trees in fan-shape—something like a view of the bowl from Charles Street looking towards Gilman Hall. A small log cabin appears as I approach the top. Suddenly the whole perspective seems filled with a fog or mist, the air is moist as after a rain, my feet are very wet and I have difficulty in breathing. I wonder what is the use of living but I insist on climbing to the top of the hill where I sink to the ground, and am awakened, by what means I do not know.

Obviously, the student can from this "dream" be convicted of sex-repression as readily as if it were a real dream.

One of the objections to dream analysis is that the dreamer in recounting the dreams, consciously or unconsciously fills up the gaps which originally existed in the dream, and thus gives us something which does not belong to the dream proper. From what has been said concerning artificial dreams, it can be seen that this makes no material difference in the analysis, for the dreamer will consciously or unconsciously gravitate towards his own strivings. This also answers those who claim that some patients treated by analysis consciously lie about their symptoms, and hence the psychanalysis is worthless. I am always pleased when a patient tells me lies. Sooner or later I usually discover the truth, and the former lies then throw some light on the neurosis. For every conscious lie, even in normal persons, is a direct or indirect wish. Like dreaming, everything that necessitates lying must be of importance to the individual concerned. Brill: Artificial Dreams and Lying. *Journal of Abnormal Psychology,* Vol. 9, 1914-15, p. 326.

The *reductio ad absurdum* of the psychoanalysis of dreams is furnished by Jung, who is the *enfant terrible* of the school.

The first three instances are from a middle-aged married man whose conflict of the moment was an extra-conjugal love affair. The piece of the dream from which I take the symbolized number is: *in front of the manager his general subscription. The manager comments on the high number of the subscription. It reads* 2477.

*   *   *   *   *   *   *   *   *   *

In this way the patient arrived at the following series of associations: [taking first the day and month, then month and year.]

He is born on .... 26 II
His mistress .... 28 VIII
His wife .... 1 III
His mother (his father is long dead) .... 26 II
His two children .... 29 IV
                                    and   13 VII
The patient is born II.75
His mistress VIII.85
He is now 36 years old, his mistress 25.

If this series of associations is written in the usual figures, the following addition is arrived at:

26.	II	=	262
28.	VIII	=	288
1.	III	=	13
26.	II	=	262
29.	IV	=	294
13.	VII	=	137
II.	75	=	275
VIII.	85	=	885
	25	=	25
	36	=	36
			2477

This series, which includes all the members of his family gives the number 2477. Jung: *Analytic Psychology*, Long's translation. p. 91.

The symbolism which the Freudians read into the dreams does actually occur in certain cases, and occurs there as a special case of the general phenomenon of association of ideas; a prosaic principle which psychology has long understood. The following dream, related by an unmarried lady approximately thirty, well illustrates this:

I seemed to be in a department store walking down an aisle between the counters on each side. Behind the counter on the left a lion was selling brilliantly colored goods—cloth of some sort. Behind the counter on the right an anchor was selling white goods.

An explanation of this dream, which is akin to the Freudian type of explanation, is plausible. The lady's brother-in-law had been for some time before this dream attempting to seduce her. Certain peculiarities of his had frequently suggested a lion to her. When questioned about the "anchor," the association of a devout woman friend was immediately brought up: a woman whose counsels and advice had had great influence on her and to whom she turned at times of trial. Further suggestions of the anchor were of something holding her back from destruction as a ship's anchor holds it. "White goods" suggested purity: the "colored goods," sex indulgence. When questioned as to previous conscious associations between the bright colors and sin, between white and chastity, she recalled many illustrations from hymns, scripture texts and sermons. Similar material with regard to an anchor was readily recalled. In other words, the "symbols" in the dream were things which had previously been associated many times over with the actual situations to which the dream pointed. Nothing is here of "unconscious libido," "subconsciousness" or "repression." Everything follows commonplace laws of association of ideas, nor was the situation to which the dream referred an unconscious one although the patient was not easily brought to the point of confessing it. This latter characteristic is true in my opinion of all the cases in which the Freudian analysis "strikes oil". The situation which is discovered through analysis is one which is perfectly well known to the patient, but the patient is loth to confess it and does not realize its importance.

The lady whose dream is above outlined had many other dreams of similar makeup. Symbols such as dried leaves, lilies, snow, blood and so on occurred, and the associations of many of these were easily recalled as having been formed by Sunday School hymns in which the symbolism was specifically embodied, as in the hymns "Whiter than Snow," and "Nothing but Leaves."*

The causation of dreams is a small and comparatively unimportant work of the total activities of the Kobold im Kellar. All the little variations from the normal routine of mental life, slips of the pen in writing, slips of the tongue in speaking, erratic and selective forgetting, odd and clumsy actions and many other details of the daily mental activities are the work of these "repressed desires." Wit and humor are addressed exclusively to the "complexes:" comic emotion is intrinsically the satisfaction which these desires obtain through round-about channels. In fact the simple and easy explanation of all the complicated activities of the mind is offered to us in one term: *repressed desires.*

An illustration of the way the complex may cause

*The analysis of dreams, which is so travested by the Freudians, is an important and interesting part of psychology. To those who have studied the subject seriously, the naive psychoanalytic "interpretations" are as amusing as the explanations children give of principles of physics. It is with reluctance that I abstain from inserting here a chapter on dreams from the scientific viewpoint; a chapter, however, which would be a serious digression.

one to forget something is given in the following instance from Freud:

Another patient spoke about a neighboring summer resort, and maintained that besides the two familiar inns there was a third. I disputed the existence of any third inn, and referred to the fact that I had spent seven summers in the vicinity and therefore knew more about the place than he. Instigated by my contradiction, he recalled the name. The name of the third inn was ''The Hochwartner.'' Of course, I had to admit it; indeed, I was forced to confess that for seven summers I had lived near this very inn whose existence I had so strenuously denied. But why should I have forgotten the name and the object? I believe because the name sounded very much like that of a Vienna colleague who practised the same specialty as my own. It touched in me the ''professional complex.'' Freud: *Psychopathology of Everyday Life*, Brill's translation, pp. 39-40.

From the same source we obtain illuminating illustrations of the way in which actions which seem to be accidental in their nature are really (according to Freud) caused by wishes which the actor does not recognize.

The effect of personal relation can be recognized also in the following examples reported by Jung. (The Psychology of Dementia Præcox, p. 45.)

Mr. Y. falls in love with a lady who soon thereafter marries Mr. X. In spite of the fact that Mr. Y. was an old acquaintance of Mr. X., and had business relations with him, he repeatedly forgot the name, and on a number of occasions, when wishing to correspond with X., he was obliged to ask other people for his name. (*op. cit.*, p. 43.)

In latter years, since I have been collecting such observations, it has happened several times that I have shattered and broken objects of some value, but the examination of these cases convinced me that it was never the result of accident or of unintentional awkwardness. Thus, one morning while in my bathrobe and straw slippers I followed a sudden impulse as I passed a room, and hurled a slipper from my foot against the wall so that it brought down a beautiful little marble Venus from its bracket. As it fell to pieces I recited quite unmoved the following verse from Busch:

> "Ach! Die Venus ist perdu—
> Klickeradoms!—von Medici!"

This crazy action and my calmness at the sight of the damage is explained in the then existing situation. We had a very sick person in the family, of whose recovery I had personally despaired. That morning I had been informed that there was a great improvement; I know that I had said to myself, "After all she will live." My attack of destructive madness served therefore as the expression of a grateful feeling toward fate, and afforded me the opportunity of performing an "act of sacrifice," just as if I had vowed, "If she gets well I will give this or that as a sacrifice." That I chose the Venus of Medici as this sacrifice was only gallant homage to the convalescent. But even today it is still incomprehensible to me that I decided so quickly, aimed so accurately, and struck no other object in close proximity. (*Op. cit.*, pp. 186-187.)

I will report exhaustively one in place of many such examples from my professional experience. A young woman broke her leg below the knee in a carriage accident so that she was bedridden for weeks. The striking part of it was the lack of any manifestation of pain and the calmness with which she bore her misfortune. This calamity ushered in a long and serious neurotic illness, from which she was finally cured by psychotherapy. During the treatment I discovered the circumstances surrounding the accident, as well as certain impressions which preceded it. The young woman with her jealous husband spent some time on the farm of her married sister, in company with her numerous other brothers and sisters with their wives and husbands. One evening she gave an exhibition of one of her talents before this intimate circle; she danced artistically the "cancan," to the great delight of her relatives, but to the great annoyance of her husband, who afterward whispered to her, "Again you have behaved like a prostitute." The words took effect. We will leave it undecided whether it was just on account of the dance. That night she was restless in her sleep, and the next forenoon she decided to go out driving. She chose the horses herself, refusing one team and demanding another. Her youngest sister wished to have her baby with its nurse accompany her, but she opposed this vehemently. During the drive she was nervous; she reminded the coachman that the horses were getting skittish, and as the fidgety animals really produced a momentary difficulty she jumped from the carriage in fright and broke her leg, while those remaining in the carriage were uninjured. Although after the disclosure of these details we can hardly doubt that this accident was really contrived, we cannot fail to admire the skill which forced the accident to mete out a punishment so suitable to the crime. For as it happened "cancan" dancing with her became impossible for a long time. *Op. cit.* pp. 199-200.

This quotation is an especially good illustration of the selective nature of psychoanalytic interpretation and of the naive ability of the psychoanalyst to close his eyes to the outstanding details of the case which do not comport with his scheme of interpretation. Perhaps also racial views on family matters are involved here. To the man who looks on the family from the German point of view it may seem quite natural that the wife who has just been crushingly insulted by the husband should meekly accept the "corrections" and have no further mental result than a wifely desire to conform to her husband's will. Hence, as a further means of carrying out that general desire, the Freudian adds the unconscious desire to so maim herself that she will be obliged to conform. It does not seem to occur to Freud that the gross insult described could produce in a woman an emotional reaction such as a man would experience under similar conditions; that the nervous excitement resulting in defective integration and faulty coordination could actually be causes of an accident. This selective interpretation is involved in a great deal of the Freudian literature.

It is a striking and generally to be recognized feature in the behavior of paranoics, that they attach the greatest significance to the trivial details in the behavior of others. Details which are usually overlooked by others they interpret and utilize as the basis of far-reaching conclusions. For example, the last paranoic seen by me concluded that there was a general understanding among people of his environment, because at this departure from the railway-station they made a certain motion with one hand. Another noticed how people walked on the street, how they brandished their walking-sticks, and the like.

(Proceeding from other points of view, this interpretation of the trivial and accidental by the patient has been designated as ''delusions of reference.'') *Op. cit.,* pp. 304-305.

This, by Freud himself, is perhaps the best description of the psychoanalytic method which has yet appeared. In this connection, the delusions of grandeur and persecution, with inordinate jealousy, naively revealed in Freud's *History of Psychoanalysis,* are striking.

When a member of my family complains that he or she has bitten his tongue, bruised her finger, and so on, instead of the expected sympathy I put the question, ''Why did you do that?'' But I have most painfully squeezed my thumb, after a youthful patient acquainted me during the treatment with his intention (naturally not to be taken seriously) of marrying my eldest daughter, while I knew that she was then in a private hospital in extreme danger of losing her life. *Op. cit.*, p. 201.

For an excellent example of this kind which was very skilfully utilized by the observer, I am indebted to Dr. Bernh. Dattner (Vienna):

I dined in a restaurant with my colleague H., a doctor of philosophy. He spoke about the injustice done to probationary students, and added that even before he finished his studies he was placed as secretary to the ambassador, or rather the extraordinary plenipotentiary Minister to Chili. "But," he added, "the minister was afterwards transferred, and I did not make any effort to meet the newly appointed." While uttering the last sentence he was lifting a piece of pie to his mouth, but he let it drop as if out of awkwardness. I immediately grasped the hidden sense of this symptomatic action, and remarked to my colleague, who was unacquainted with psychoanalysis, "You really allowed a very choice morsel to slip from you." He did not realize, however, that my words could equally refer to his symptomatic action, and he repeated the same words I uttered with a peculiarly agreeable and surprising vividness, as if I had actually taken the words from his mouth. "It was really a very choice morsel that I allowed to get away from me." He then followed this remark with a detailed description of his clumsiness, which had cost him this very remunerative position.

The sense of this symbolic action becomes clearer if we remember that my colleague had scruples about telling me, almost a perfect stranger, concerning his precarious material situation, and his repressed thought took on the mask of symptomatic action which expressed symbolically what was meant to be concealed, and the speaker thus got relief from his unconscious. *Op. cit.*, pp. 232-233.

One wonders how the analysis would have been changed if the agitation of H. had caused him to

drop cigar ashes on his coat, or knock over a glass
of water, instead of dropping his pie.

Chance or symptomatic actions occurring in affairs of married
life have often a most serious significance, and could lead those
who do not concern themselves with the psychology of the unconscious to a belief in omens. It is not an auspicious beginning if
a young woman loses her wedding-ring on her wedding-day, even
if it were only mislaid and soon found.

I know a woman, now divorced, who in the management of her
business affairs frequently signed her maiden name many years
before she actually resumed it. *Op. cit.*, pp. 235-236.

Brill reports the following example: A doctor took exception
to the following statement in my book, ''We never lose what we
really want'' (*Psychanalysis, its Theories and Practical Application*, p. 214). His wife, who is very interested in psychologic subjects, read with him the chapter on ''Psychopathology of Everyday Life;'' they were both very much impressed with the novelty of
the ideas, and so on, and were very willing to accept most of the
statements. He could not, however, agree with the above-given
statement because, as he said to his wife, ''I surely did not wish
to lose my knife.'' He referred to a valuable knife given to him
by his wife, which he highly prized, the loss of which caused him
much pain.

It did not take his wife very long to discover the solution for
this loss in a manner to convince them both of the accuracy of my
statement. When she presented him with this knife he was a bit
loath to accept it. Although he considered himself quite emanci-
pated, he nevertheless entertained some superstition about giving
or accepting a knife as a gift, because it is said that a knife cuts
friendship. He even remarked this to his wife, who only laughed
at his superstition. He had the knife for years before it disappeared.

Analysis brought out the fact that the disappearance of the
knife was directly connected with a period when there were violent
quarrels between himself and his wife, which threatened to end
in separation. They lived happily together until his step-daughter

(it was his second marriage) came to live with them. His daughter was the cause of many misunderstandings, and it was at the height of these quarrels that he lost the knife.

The unconscious activity is very nicely shown in this symptomatic action. In spite of his apparent freedom from superstition, he still unconsciously believed that a donated knife may cut friendship between the persons concerned. The losing of it was simply an unconscious defence against losing his wife, and by sacrificing the knife he made the superstitious ban impotent. *Op. cit.*, pp. 241-242.

Brill tells of a woman who, inquiring about a mutual friend, erroneously called her by her maiden name. Her attention having been directed to this error, she had to admit that she disliked her friend's husband and had never been satisfied with her marriage. (*Op. cit.*, p. 258.)*

The similarity between anecdotal evidence of the sort adduced from the preceding quotation and the anecdotal evidence on which the spiritualists and telepathists depend is striking. The incident quoted might be paraphrased as follows: Blank tells of a woman who had a dream in which a former friend of hers committed suicide. Two days later the friend actually did commit suicide. A conclusive proof of the veridical nature of dreams! The essential character of this anecdotal evidence is its selectiveness, already pointed out in connection with the anecdote of the lady who Freud supposed broke her leg from an unconscious purpose. The particular inference which was prepared in

*This, of course, may well be an illustration of the tendency to forget the mildly unpleasant which is well founded, independently of Freudian principles, on the general principles of association.

advance is extracted from the vaguely defined situation the anecdote covers, regardless of other equally plausible inferences and the lack of sufficient analysis for any reliable inference. This method of "wish-fulfillment" so characteristic of Freudian and occultist literature, is properly described as *arbitrary inference*.

An application of the Freudian principles might very well be made to the explanation of a phenomenon which has puzzled a great many persons. It is well known that a man has a tendency to whistle, sing, or make a noise which he supposes to be singing while taking a bath. Even the quietest, mildest man when under the shower or in the tub may become afflicted with the idea that he is a song-bird. Now we may well suppose that the water in which he is wholly or partly immersed symbolizes here, as everywhere else in psychoanalysis, the amniotic fluid in which the pre-natal life was spent. Getting into the water, by the conventional Freudian method of reversal, symbolizes being born, as well as the desire to return to the intrauterine conditions of life. The infant immediately after birth yells lustily; the noises made by the man therefore symbolize his infantile desire to undo the work of parturition, and return to the mother. The phenomenon therefore is merely the representation of the unconscious libido fixed on the mother: the Oedipus complex. I offer this interpretation to the

Freudians for what it is worth. The reason why we eat fruit at the beginning of breakfast, but at the end of dinner, might also be explained as a "subconscious" harking back to the blissful condition of our long-tailed ancestors, who, returning to the trees for the night after foraging miscellaneously on the ground, topped off with some fruit there, and again indulged before descending in the morning.

Clearly in the Freudian system appears the fundamental anti-scientific postulate of mysticism: a form of knowledge—consciousness—which yet is not consciousness, something which, when it is convenient for the purposes of argument, can be given the attributes and qualities of consciousness, but which when these attributes are inconvenient is entirely divested of them. To this mystic knowledge in the Freudian system, as in that of philosophical mysticism, is ascribed an importance far above that of consciousness itself. The essential difference in the two theories is that whereas the philosophical mystics ascribe a purely intuitive value to ecstasy or union, the Freudians in addition to the enormous intuitive importance—the unconscious includes a knowledge of all the experiences through which the race has passed—ascribe to it definite and practical physiological consequences. In comparison with philosophical mysticism then, psychoanalysis stands out not so much as a mere variation on a theme as a gigantic expansion of it.

The foundation on which the whole of psychoanalysis rests is the theory of the unconscious. Under this, however, is not to be understood a term derived from abstract thought nor merely an hypothesis created with the aim of establishing a philosophic system; with the significance, for example, which Eduard von Hartmann has given the word, psychoanalysis possesses no connection at all. The negative peculiarity of the phenomenon appearing in the term, namely, the absence of the quality of consciousness, is indeed the most essential and most characteristic one, but not, however, the only one. We are already familiar with a whole series of positive distinguishing features which differentiate the unconscious psychic material from the rest, the conscious and foreconscious.

An idea which at a given moment belongs to the content of consciousness of an individual, can in the next moment have disappeared; others, emerging later, have appeared in its place. Nevertheless, the idea still retains a permanent relation to the conscious mental life, for it can be brought back again by some kind of connected association chain without the necessity of a new sense perception; that is to say, in the interim, the idea was removed from the conscious mental life but still remained accessible to the mental processes. Such ideas, which indeed lack the quality of consciousness, the latter being every time recoverable however, we call the foreconscious and distinguish this most explicitly from the real unconscious.

The real unconscious ideas are not, like the foreconscious ideas, temporarily separated from the conscious mental life, but are permanently excluded from it; the power to reenter consciousness, or stated more exactly, the normal waking consciousness of the subject, these ideas lack completely. As the state of consciousness changes, so also does its condition of receptivity. Rank and Sachs: *The Significance of Psychoanalysis for the Mental Sciences*, Payne's Translation, p. 1.

The separation of the "unconscious" from the

"conscious" is not however so complete as this statement seems to imply. The authors proceed to answer the question: "To what peculiarities do the unconscious ideas owe the fact that the quality of consciousness is withheld from them with such stubbornness? Wherein rests their incompatibility with the other psychic forces?" (p. 3) and proceed to expand the details of the relationship. The distinction between unconscious and foreconscious is not clearly maintained, and a great deal of what is said about the unconscious may be intended to apply to the foreconscious. The distinction is not generally made by other writers.

Our first question will naturally concern the origin of the unconscious. Since the unconscious stands completely foreign and unknown to the conscious personality, the first impulse would be to deny connection with consciousness in general. This is the manner in which the folk-belief has even been treated of. The bits of the unconscious which were visible in abnormal mental states passed as proof of "being possessed," that is, they were conceived as expressions of a strange individual, of a demon, who had taken possession of the patient. We, who can no longer rely on such supernatural influences, must seek to explain the facts psychologically. The hypothesis that a primary division of the psychic life exists from birth, contradicts the experience of the continual conflict between the two groups of forces, since if the separation were present from the beginning, the danger of a shifting of boundaries would not exist. The only possible assumption, which is further confirmed by experience, is that the separation does not exist *a priori*, but originates only in the course of time. This demarcation of the boundary line must be a process which ends before the complete attainment of the normal level of culture; thus, we may say it begins in earliest childhood and has found a temporary termination about the time of puberty. The unconscious originates in the childhood of man, which circumstance affords the explanation for most of its peculiarities. Rank and Sachs: *op. cit.*, p. 3.

Jung's explanation of the subconscious is based on his conception of Leibnitz,

When we speak of a thing as being unconscious we must not forget that from the point of view of the functioning of the brain, a thing may be unconscious in two ways,—physiologically or psychologically. I shall only deal with the subject from the latter point of view, so that for our purposes we may define the unconscious as "the sum of all those psychological events which are not apperceived and so are unconscious."

The unconscious contains all those psychic events, which because of the lack of the necessary intensity of their functioning are unable to pass the threshold which divides the conscious from the unconscious, so that they remain in effect below the surface of the conscious and slip by in subliminal, phantom form. It has been known to psychologists since the time of Leibnitz that the elements, that is to say, the ideas and feelings which go to make up the conscious mind, the so-called conscious content, are of a complex nature and rest upon far simpler and altogether unconscious elements. It is the combination of these which give the element of consciousness. *Analytical Psychology*, Chap. X, Long's translation, p. 278. We must be satisfied with the definition already given, which will prove quite sufficient for our purposes, namely: the conception of the unconscious as the sum of all the psychological processes below the threshold of consciousness. *Analytic Psychology*, p. 279. Now we know that a certain section of the unconscious contains all our lost memories and also all those unfortunate impulses which cannot find any application in adult life. *Analytic Psychology*, p. 372.

Like its parent, psychoanalysis is essentially antagonistic to scientific psychology and scientific method in the mental sciences. Scientific psychology is entirely destroyed by an admixture of mysticism because both the purposes and the methods of the science are rendered futile. When by mere application of *a priori* principles an emotionally satisfactory explanation of the universe can be obtained without the baffling labor of scientific analysis and experimentation, obviously, scientific methods will not be applied.

The psychoanalyst like the philosophical mystic is essentially tender-minded, and cannot endure the difficulties and disappointments of prosaic science.* We are not surprised, therefore, to find over and above the essential logical fallacy on which the system is based, a characteristic naiveté in reasoning and a characteristic lack of orientation in facts. This is beautifully brought out in Riklin's *Wish Fulfillment and Symbolism in Fairy Tales.* Riklin, by the application of Freudian principles to fairy tales, deduces a very serious conclusion which, he remarks, his readers will be loath to admit because it is so revolutionary; and which he apparently be-

---

*In connection with what is said here and later concerning the motives which impel various individuals to adopt Freudianism, we should not lose sight of a more practical motive which is undoubtedly dominant in many cases, namely, the easy financial reward of psychoanalytic practice. After a study of Freudianism which may be very superficial, the psychoanalyst, especially if provided with a medical degree, can begin on a very lucrative practice, although his training may have included little psychiatry and less psychology. Physicians in general practice are finding that psychoanalysis is a good "side line" which requires only the preliminary acquisition of the lingo and the leading of the patient into the ever-interesting topic of sex. It is fair to say that the more serious followers of Freud deplore this "wild" psychoanalysis, although the results of the operations of the "wild" practitioners are not noticeably different from those of the regulars.

lieves could have been discovered only by deduc-
tion from the Freudian hypothesis. This startling
conclusion is that the interest taken by children
(and adults) in fairy tales is *wish fulfillment*.
Taking Cinderella as an example, he finds that girls
are interested in the tale because they would like
to go to balls, they would like to wear wonderful
gowns, they would like to have handsome princes
try slippers on them, they would like to live happy
ever after.* One is somewhat dazed on first pe-
rusal of this remarkable monograph. One wonders
how there can be intelligent people to whom this
explanation is any surprise. I have made careful
inquiry, since reading Riklin's impressive statement, of many intelligent adults and small children,
and so far have found no one who doubted the reality of the desires, the adequacy of the explanation, or who needed any application of Freudian
principles to discover it. (I have not so far carried
the investigation to individuals below the grade of
moron.

---

*In an equally naive way the Freudians deduce from time to time other
important "discoveries" from the Freudian principles. The great importance
of sex in human life is something which is supposed to have been entirely
unknown until pointed out by Freud. It is a constant surprise to disciples
of the Vienna physician that a psychologist may recognize, and even empha-
size, the fundamental role which sex ideas and sex activities play in mind
and conduct and yet not be a Freudian. Even the principles of the association of ideas, are, by frequent implication, products of psychoanalysis. The
fact that all the details of conscious conduct are causally directed by the results of previous experience was, according to psychoanalysis, never sur-
mised until Freud's *Psychopathology of Everyday Life* appeared. Students
unacquainted with psychology, who get their first knowledge of commonplace
psychological facts from Freudian sources, necessarily look upon Freud as
the founder of modern mental science.

The essential point of difference between the facts and Riklin's marvelous discovery is that these desires in adults and in children are perfectly conscious and recognized, showing no signs of "repression."

The use of the mystic postulate, by removing the discussion from the galling restrictions of logic makes explanation very easy. The standard psychoanalytic explanation of action and of consciousness alike is that they arise from the unconscious (or foreconscious or subconscious). If this term is taken in a definite sense, the explanation disappears, since it means nothing more than that the activities and the consciousness of human individuals are dependent on physiological processes: or else it means that the activities arise in consciousness, leaving the causes without explanation. To be more specific; an unconscious wish either is an unconscious physiological process, in which case it is not a wish: or else it really is a wish, in which case it is conscious. Consider the case of Abbe Oegger as explained by Jung: This priest, whose story is related by Anatole France in *Le Jardin d'Epicure,* believed that Judas was not eternally damned, but because he had been chosen by God in his all wisdom as the instrument through which an important work was done, he was pardoned. He asked for, and received a sign from God that his assumption was correct; then went about preaching the Gospel of the all-merciful. Finally, he separated from the Church and became a Swedenborgian.

Now we understand his Judas phantasy. *He was the Judas who betrayed his Lord.* Therefore, first of all, he had to make sure of the divine mercy, in order to be a Judas in peace. Jung: *Psychology of the Unconscious,* Hinkle's Translation, pp. 39-40.

Assuming Jung to mean that Oegger's action was due to his unconscious wish to be a Judas we may ask; did he have such a wish or did he not? If by "wish" we mean something which we define from our own experience, Oegger either had a conscious wish or no wish at all. The Freudians' claim that there can be a wish that is not a wish, is the making of a claim that there is something other than the wish of ordinary experience, which they will insist on calling nevertheless a wish; and which really has no connotation except the connotation derived from the wish of conscious experience. In reality the "unconscious wish" is an indeterminate something akin to the mathematician's $\frac{0}{0}$ which symbol ought to be used in every case where the psychoanalysts use the terms unconscious, foreconscious, or subconscious.* It is quite obvious that the Freudians call this unknown $\frac{0}{0}$ a "wish" because they find it advantageous to treat

---

*If "wish," and all other emotional facts were defined as merely physiological facts, we might say that there are wishes of which we are not conscious, just as there are bricks of which we are not conscious. But with such definition, the Freudian system falls to pieces.

it now as if it were really a wish (a conscious motive for action in Oegger's case) : and they call it "unconscious" because it is convenient to treat it again as if it were something else than the wish (when for example it is asked whether Oegger really had such a wish.)

The false reasoning consequent on this use of an important term in two different significances is the well known logical *fallacy of ambiguous middle*: one of the devices most favored by all the great company of slipshod thinkers. By emphasizing now one meaning, now another meaning, of the term, dubious transitions may be made with ease, and a principle may be applied over a much wider range than exact logic would permit.

If, as Jevons remarks, we argue that "all metals are elements and brass is a metal, therefore, it is an element," we should be using the middle term "metal" in two different senses, in one of which it means the pure simple substances known to chemists as metals, and in the other, a mixture of metals commonly called metal in the arts, but known to chemists by the name "alloy." Or, if we argue that "what is right should be enforced by law, and that charity is right and should be enforced by law," it is evident that "right" is applied in one case to what the conscience approves, and in another use to what public opinion holds to be necessary for the good of society.* Davies: *Text-Book of Logic,* p. 535.

---

*The use of the sliding term—the fallacy of the ambiguous middle term—creeps into and poisons scientific reasoning wherever rigorous logical watchfulness is relaxed. One of the most flagrant examples outside of Freudianism of this unfortunate lapse is the well known argument for what is known in the "all or none law" as applied to nerve cells: that is, the theory that a neuron acts ("discharges"), when it acts at all, with the full energy of action of which it is capable at the time, being, according to the theory,

The result of the fallacy of ambiguous middle as employed by the Freudian in such cases is that it gives a specious explanation, comforting to his demand for easy but final knowledge, and relieving him of any tendency to seek for actual scientific explanation. Let us see how the mystical resolution of problems by the use of "trick" terms obscures the possibility of real solution. Probably the eventual act of the priest described by Anatole France was not independent of his doctrinal analysis of the Judas problem. Whether both acts were expressive of a growing liberalism in faith, or whether the solution of the first problem in itself inclined him to the second step, is a problem which cannot be solved on the basis of the slender evidence presented in the case: but the willingness to shut one's eyes to the problem is unquestionably a willingness to accept the arbitrary interpretation

---

somewhat analogous to a powder-fuse, which, if it is lighted, burns completely. What is actually shown is that the neuron resists poisoning in an "all or none" way: that when being slowly poisoned, it continues to act with normal efficiency up to the point at which it suddenly ceases altogether to act. From this "all or none" principle is then inferred a totally different "all or none" law, namely: that the neuron, in its normal or unpoisoned condition either acts (discharges) with all its energy, or not at all. This is precisely as if one should observe a man in a boat, fighting against the wind and waves with all his energy up to the moment at which he drops dead from heart failure, and should infer therefrom that the man, while living, was unable to row with varying degrees of energy, but could only put forth his full energy or none at all.

In modern psychology, the central fallacy of the old Anglo-German psychology still lingers: the fallacy from which spring both Freudianism and what is known as "behaviorism." This fallacy is the use of the term "consciousness" (with the cognate terms "sensation," "thought" and "feeling") to designate both *awareness,* and *that of which* there is awareness. Through the confusion of these two meanings under one term, the progress of mental science has been much hindered: no psychology which includes this confusion can hope to be scientific.

in order to avoid the disagreeable fact that much more information and difficult scientific labor would be needed in order to arrive at a conclusion of any value: the shrinking of a tender mind from the hard conditions of actuality into the shadowy realm of fable. The psychoanalyst's procedure is in truth adequately expressed in his own terms as *wish fulfillment*.

The anti-scientific attitude of the psychoanalyst is not something casual which has come about through mere looseness of expression or temporary confusion such as occurs in the best intentioned scientific process—all scientists do fall from grace from time to time. Hinkle, for example, plants her feet squarely and resolutely in the quicksand in saying:

This term ''unconscious'' is used very loosely in Freudian psychology and is not intended to provoke any academic* discussion, but to conform strictly to the dictionary classification of a negative concept which can neither be described nor defined. To say that an idea of feeling is unconscious merely means to indicate that the individual is unaware at that time of its existence, or that all the material of which he is unaware at a given time is unconscious. Hinkle, B., in Introduction to Jung: *Psychology of the Unconscious*, p. xv.

The Practical Results of Psychoanalysis

The fact that cures may be performed through the technique associated with the theories of psy-

---

*"Academic" is the term usually applied by tender-minded theorizers to the practical logicians who try to pin them down to a definite meaning.

choanalysis, is of course no proof of the truth of the theories. Christian Science, hypnotism, osteopathy, relics of saints and the laying on of hands also produced cures. We may be more liberal in our estimation than are the devotees of these various sects, and admit that each of them at times accomplishes good results, although none of them may admit the fact in regard to the others. However estimable pragmatism may be as a theory of knowledge, the incomplete evidence of the way a certain treatment "works" on neurotic patients is more theoretical than pragmatic. Conversely, the faulty foundations of the technique are not in themselves absolute assurance that the technique will not produce desirable results in some cases.

* * * Psychoanalysis has actually been applied to the treatment of nervous diseases, and a large number of writers have reported the success they have obtained. No one dreams of doubting these cures which are, fortunately, frequent in the practice of psychotherapy whatever may be the method employed or the convictions of the physician. The temple of Æsculapius has cured thousands of patients, Lourdes has cured thousands of patients, animal magnetism has cured thousands of patients, Christian Science has cured thousands of patients, hypnotic suggestion has cured thousands of patients, and psychoanalysis has cured thousands of patients; these are incontestable facts. But, if I dare to speak my thoughts, this fact, interesting as it may be to the patients who are cured, has no great interest for the physician. What is interesting to us is the patients who are not cured, who implore our help, and the important question is to know if we can apply to them with some hope of success the treatment which has been so successful with others. It is not enough to be told that a patient has been cured by being plunged into the holy water, or by relating in great detail his first masturbation; the determining cause which unites the symptoms of the neurosis must also be made clear, and it must be proved that it was the bath or the confession which brought about a cure. Now that does not seem to me to be easy to prove; passing over the difficulty of verifying cures of this kind, it is extremely difficult to eliminate other influences which may have modified the disease. The greater number of neuropaths are suggestible persons, suffering from fatigue and weakness, and often the treatment has been accompanied by a change of *régime*, physical and moral relaxation, and strong suggestion. These patients above all else suffer from depression, and this depression is relieved by all the causes of stimulation which accompany the treatment. They are happy because some one is occupied with them, that a new method of treatment is applied to them, a disputed treatment, strange and a trifle shocking in its apparent disdain of customary modesty. They are flattered that the observations made upon them serve to establish a medical method which is to cure all the ills of human kind; they experience a legitimate pride in the thought that they are collaborating with a great man in the reconstruction of medicine. Many patients before now have found a cure in animal magnetism because the long *séances*, the seeking for singular procedures and marvelous benefits, and the aspirations towards greater clearness gave an occupation to their lives and fed their imagination and vanity. If, by chance, such influences, unknown to the observer, have played a part in the cures which have been reported to us, are we certain of being able to obtain such cures again by applying solely the rules given by the Freudian school, but without adding to them the modifications of *régime*, rest, suggestion and stimulation which these observers have forgotten to speak of? This is why it is not very useful to report to physicians the thousands of cures that have been obtained, and why the physiological and psychological mechanism of these cures should be indicated with greater precision; also the reasons for supposing that such or such a well-defined practice has been beneficial. Janet: Psychoanalysis, *Journal of Abnormal Psychology*, Vol. IX, 1914-15, p. 180.

It is probable that psychoanalysts do produce cures, or at least marked alleviation of the condition, of certain cases. In other cases the results are less desirable. The question of vital importance is whether the harm done by the general application of the method outweighs the good accomplished.

We may assume, in order to be as liberal as possible, that there are some neuroses whose causes bear some resemblance to the schematic "complexes" of the psychoanalytic system. In other words, the psychoanalyst's description of the etiology of these cases may be taken as an allegorical, but not entirely mistaken, account. Such cases which, on a conservative scheme of classification, may be designated as a satyristic, nymphomaniac. or of perversion, may respond to the treatment. In certain other cases a complex corresponding to the allegorical description is built up by prolonged psychoanalysis. The patient, for example, is convinced that his neurosis is a result of the mother-complex; at first he is astonished at the psychoanalyst's discovery but by the copious use of symbolism, by the perversion of all the patient says and does, with that end in view, he is finally persuaded that the complex originated in him, and not in the psychoanalyst. By constant contemplation of the complex and its magic relationships, all the symptoms of the patient's troubles become closely associated with it. If now the psychoanalyst can exorcise the demon he has raised the patient may be cured. He has followed an ancient prescription and thrown the patient into fits; then cured the fits.* The difficulty arises in the curing of the fits. It is not impossible that the process may be carried through to completion. A system of ideas with definite emotional setting may be made temporarily habitual, with the definite expectation and certainty on the part of the patient that he is to be ultimately rid of them. In many cases, however, the demon refuses to be exorcised or if he complacently leaves, returns shortly with "seven worse than himself," and the latter state of the patient is worse than the first.

It is apparently possible to restore by scientific treatment a patient who has been given a mother-complex by psychoanalysis; but the restoration is certainly a difficult process and the prognosis of the patient far less encouraging than for a patient who has not had psychoanalytic "help."

It is probable that with the majority of candidates for psychoanalysis the complex is not developed in any serious sense. The patient craves the personal interest of the psychoanalyst or other practitioner and accepts in a superficial way any

---

*It is to be understood of course that this description of the process of cure is a figurative one, following psychoanalytic models. A more exact description of what actually takes place in the patient when he is thus made the nursery for a complex destined for the slaughter, may easily be constructed.

suggestion made by the sympathetic listener, provided these suggestions have a certain flavor of profundity and are vehicles of hope. In this respect Christian Science, psychoanalysis and the thousand and one other techniques for whose operations the neurotics are the natural prey, present no essential differences. The confessional of the church achieves the same result in a more scientific way.

How much benefit in total percentage is achieved by the various treatments which coddle the neurotic is a question concerning which little reliable information is at hand. One cannot help but feel that for these patients whose chief trouble is self-pity, anything but the coddling treatment would be preferable. Possibly a purely social rather than an individualistic view of neuroses would help, since after all the neurotic is a social problem. This, however, is not the place to expound a detailed constructive view on this point. Aside from the effect on the specific neurotic patient, the effect on society at large produced by the dissemination of mystic medicine ought to be considered. This is a psychological problem although not the specific psychological problem whose discussion we are involved in. It is a part of the general problem of the circulation of pornographic literature complicated, however, by the circumstance that a bolder front is put upon the salacious propaganda by the label of "psychology" or "science." In this respect Freudianism "has it over" Boccacio, the Arabian Nights and Balzac. Certainly the inculcation of Freudian principles should not be permitted to reach the very young, or the ignorant, any more than should obscene prints.

Concerning "repression" there are certain important observations which should be made, although these observations do not strictly pertain to our general critique of the Freudian system. There is a psychological fact which corresponds in a rudimentary way to the mystical "repression." In the first place things which are now "in consciousness" may be in a few moments forgotten. We are constantly forgetting things and in many cases this forgetting is aided and accelerated by voluntary processes. In common language: we try to forget and this trying is sometimes efficacious.

We do not, of course, suppose that what is forgotten still exists, in the same form as before, but stored in an "unconscious warehouse" of the mind. An idea is not a thing like a written document which, after being in the active files is taken out and stored in the transfer case. It is more like an *act* such as snapping the fingers or striking a blow. I may snap my fingers ten times in succession: but no one supposes that the snaps have an individual existence afterwards and are somewhere stored away as snaps which are no longer snapping. No more does scientific psychology conceive of "ideas" as something which can be stored away after they are through "ideating." In the one case as in the other, there is a physiological basis which is modified by the act in such a way that the act can be repeated at a future time.

The things which we try to forget, and to a certain extent which we do succeed in forgetting, most readily are those which are disagreeable. The "obliviscence of the disagreeable" is a concept which is familiar in psychology although the name may have been recently applied. This obliviscence is the safety valve which prevents us from mentally "blowing up." If we could not to a large extent forget the disagreeable factors the human race would probably find existence insupportable.

The question how far the forgetting of the disagreeable is desirable is a question which depends upon the particular disagreeable. If it is a matter of inability to pay the rent, and one must call upon the landlord tomorrow to negotiate a few days' extension, it would be unfortunate to forget the matter entirely: but if one, after making determination as to the action, can forget the situation until tomorrow comes, he is thereby a gainer. If he bears it in mind during the day he not only adds nothing to his efficiency in persuading the landlord, but he also interferes with every other duty and gets himself into an unsatisfactory mental condition.

If the disagreeable matter is entirely one of the past, as in the case of an unfortunate remark, the quicker and more complete the forgetting the better. The person who is constantly remembering, and consequently feeling shame or other disagreeable emotion, over events of the past, is in an unfortunate and even dangerous predicament.

In the case of desires (in the strict sense of the word) which cannot be actualized, the situation is of more importance, but the general solution is not intrinsically different from that of the general problems of the disagreeable. Repression is the goal which must be attained, although the technique of repression may involve a certain amount of active attention to the desire. Suppose an individual has a desire for sex relation with a specific individual who is forbidden to him by social conventions, or by law, or by his ethical convictions, or by physical restraint. Constant brooding over or contemplation of the desire is mentally disturbing and physically malevolent. The best thing is to turn the attention to other matters and not dwell consciously upon the object of desire, in other words, to eliminate the desire and substitute other activities therefor. Apparently, where desire has considerable power and lastingness, a brief period of attention to it *in association with the expectation and determination* to repress it, helps the consequent repression. This is particularly efficacious when the social influences of another person's suggestion and of the social power of an institution are brought into the situation. The mechanics of this are only in part clearly known, but the facts have long been understood and the church has made powerful use thereof in the confessional. The Freudians, Christian Scientists and other psychotherapeutists make use of the same principle, although the technique of the church is probably more scientifically grounded. Sin, in short, is most dangerous when one broods over it or worries over it. A brief period of attention to it in the light of the expectation of its absolution may help in the practical absolution.

So far we have been following lines of psychological analysis which are rather general. I may add to this an expression of personal opinion which is offered as a suggestion towards a more thoroughgoing understanding of neuroses. From an examination of living cases as well as from reading the cases reported in Freudian and psychiatric literature, I am convinced that the more important causes of neuroses are not to be found in ideas of sex but rather in pathological sex activity.* The

---

*Freud, like many other psychiatrists, was friendly to this view in his early period. He and his school have completely repudiated it, however. See Jung: *The Theory of Psychoanalysis.* I do not endorse Freud's early views, but merely point out that in his earlier writings he was far less wild than in his later theories.

causes of neuroses in women seem to have a different ordering from the causes in men. At least the details of causation are not so clear in regard to the female, and hence what I have to say applies specifically to the male neurosis and not so definitely to the female.

A very frequent feature in the history of the male neurotic is irregular sex experience commencing often at a very early age. Intercourse with sisters, cousins or girl playmates is a prevalent detail. Homosexual and masturbational episodes play an important role also, and so do perverted relations of a heterosexual kind (cunnilingus and hetero-masturbation). In all these situations morbid emotion is involved. Fear is of course a prominent factor; both fear of discovery and in some cases at least fear of conception. In addition to this fear there is a deadly abnormality in the course of the sex excitement itself which, partly because of the fear, partly because of the furtiveness and haste of the procedure, does not run its normal course of crescendo and diminuendo, but is unduly accelerated and violently terminated, and throughout has not the proper coordination with the specific physiological sex activity. These abnormalities we know are powerfully pathogenic in the adult, and undoubtedly are even more so in a susceptible child or adolescent.

Another pathogenic factor which enters into a

very large number of cases occurs in the copulation with prostitutes which enters into the histories of so many neuroses. For some individuals this form of sex activity is not productive of pathological emotion. For these individuals the total situation in regard to a prostitute is not different from the situation with any other woman. These are individuals whose emotional life remains in a rather low stage of development and who are therefore immune to neuroses.

To the man of more complex susceptibility the prostitute while physiologically attractive in a certain sense is also repulsive. In some cases the lack of physical cleanliness, or the low mental and emotional level are the source of the dissatisfaction: in others ethical or aesthetic considerations connected with the type of relationship or the surroundings are more important. In all cases (for men of this type) there is a profound inadequacy in the relationship, which is in part due to the conditions under which it must be assumed, and to the same interference of the normal course of emotion which occurs in the irregularities and perversions of the youthful illicit experiences above described. One individual whose incipient neurosis I suspected to be partly due to this particular source expressed the feeling very nicely, on being questioned, in the following way: he described the harlot with whom he had been having relations as an attractive and intelligent girl, very clean and with a certain charm. ''She's perfectly all right—but oh, hell!'' This emotional antagonism amounts in many cases to a definite, although temporary, splitting of personality in its vital emotional foundation: and when there is added to it the powerful effects of disturbed and interrupted course of the sex emotion, the combination is one which can be confidently expected to unsettle the nervous integration of a delicate organization—and it does so in many cases.

Such significant factors in the possible etiology of sex neuroses are entirely ignored by psychoanalysis because of the *a priori* scheme of explanation to which they are not contributory. This is the sort of danger which mysticism constantly involves when it is applied to problems of real life.

CHAPTER III

THE FOUNDATIONS OF SCIENTIFIC PSYCHOLOGY

There are certain fundamental points of method which must be observed in all scientific procedure, and upon which Scientific Psychology is founded. FIRST: science must start from an empirical basis of the facts of experience, and must constantly correlate its processes and its productions with these facts. Psychology in particular, needs constantly to be reminding itself of this rule, since it is easy to pass from empirical psychology into philosophical speculations in which concepts are considered so abstractly that there is insufficient check on their transformation into systems which have but vague connections with assignable facts.

SECOND: science must form *working hypotheses* into which the observed facts will fit, and which therefore "explain" the facts without distorting them. These hypotheses are not to be considered as final, but are held constantly subject to correction, expansion, or replacement, according as the discovery of new facts, or the better analysis of facts already known, requires such changes.

The working hypotheses of science must be as

112

few, and as general as possible: where one hypothesis will cover all the given set of facts, that hypothesis is *ipso facto* more adequate than a rival hypothesis which takes in only a part of the facts, requiring a supplementary hypothesis to complete its scope. This rule—of the economy of hypothesis —is known as the *law of parsimony*, and is the ultimate principle in the evaluation of hypotheses. Science always prefers the simplest hypotheses, and refuses to construct a new hypothesis where one already established may be extended to cover the ground.

For example: if the hypothesis of three primary colors, whose combinations in varying proportions give rise to all the visible hues and saturations, will adequately explain the discoverable facts of normal and abnormal color vision, that theory must be preferred over a theory which assumes six primary colors and necessitates an additional hypothesis of reversible sensory action, the additional hypothesis not being required for any other physiological or psychological purposes.

THIRD: the working hypothesis of science must be subjected to experimental investigation in so far as that is possible. The constructive modification of a hypothesis, to make it fit the facts more closely, is brought about by putting it to the experimental test. The hypothesis is examined in order to determine what further facts, as yet not observed, may be logically predictable from it. Then, on arranging the conditions in such a way as to conform to these particular features of the hypothesis, the facts will either be found, or will not be found. In the former case, the hypothesis is so far verified; in the latter case, the hypothesis must be modified. This is the *experimental method*.

For an illustration of the experimental method we may again refer to the problem of color vision. There are two types of color blindness which are common, both of which are characterized by certain confusions of greens and reds. If two individuals, one belonging to each type, be given assortments of colored worsteds to arrange according to their color resemblances, the arrangements made by both men will be erroneous to the normal eye, and the arrangement made by the one man will appear erroneous to the other. From the three-color hypothesis, it may be deducted that one arrangement will appear correct to the normal eye when it is illuminated by daylight from which only a band of yellowish green has been removed: and that the other arrangement will appear correct if illuminated by daylight from which only the red has been removed. The *experiment* then consists in arranging the illumination as described, and the results being found to agree with the prediction from the hypothesis, the hypothesis is so far (but so far only) confirmed.

FOURTH: verified hypotheses, or verified details
of hypotheses, must be guaranteed by *proof*: and
scientific *proof* is a definite method which is
sharply distinguishable from historical proof or
proof in the popular sense.

When a new discovery is made in science: that is
to say, when a newly formed hypothesis is verified:
the statement of the discoverer, that such and such
a phenomenon has occurred, has in itself no scientific value. The discoverer must formulate the experimental conditions under which the phenomenon
described may be observed by any one whose scientific training has been adequate.

Some years ago an eminent chemist reported
that he had succeeded in transmuting lead into
helium. This report carried no conviction, in spite
of the untarnished reputation of the chemist, because the same result could not be obtained by other
chemists. Later the source of the error was found.
The discovery of radio-activity, on the other hand,
was certified when the conditions were laid down
under which a physicist of a certain degree of
training and with the proper apparatus could himself observe the described phenomenon. It is not
necessary that the phenomenon shall be observable
even by the trained physicist without the stipulated
apparatus and surrounding conditions.

The observance of the principles of scientific
proof is of especial importance in psychology.

Adherence to its requirements excludes the *anecdotal method* which is so copiously exemplified in spiritualism and in psychoanalysis. The mere statement that such and such a thing happened in a particular case under certain circumstances, is inconclusive because one can never be certain either that the description of the circumstances is sufficiently comprehensive; that is, that certain important details are not omitted from the account: or else that certain details specified in the account are not erroneously recollected. Such is the effect of the known fallibility of human testimony. Furthermore, we must guard against the frequent source of error in reasoning which we have described earlier as *selective reasoning,* or the drawing of a preconceived conclusion from experiments or observations which are so vaguely conditioned that a variety of inferences are as a matter of fact possible.

FIFTH: throughout the operations of scientific method, extreme care must be paid to the significance of terms. All terms must be defined with a precision adequate to the use that is to be made of them in further discussion. The use of a term which has ambiguity, if the ambiguity concerns the details which enter into the discussion, is fatal to science. The fallacy of the *ambiguous middle term* is a pit which is continuously before us and which must be strenuously avoided. Of this necessity, philosophical mysticism and psychoanalysis furnish us alarming evidence.

The ambiguities of the term *consciousness, sensation, thought, feeling,* and *perception* have been a serious matter in the past, and the poisonous influence of these ambiguities has not entirely disappeared, even from that psychology which has remained free from mystical tendencies. "Consciousness" has a variety of meanings, but has been most commonly used in two, namely, to indicate *awareness,* and the objects *of which* one is directly aware. These two meanings have been confused and employed interchangeably, so that the fallacy of the ambiguous middle term runs riot through many psychological texts. "Sensation," "thought," and "perception" have been used as terms indicating species of this "consciousness," so that the confusion has extended to them in the same degree. Blue as seen, is called a "sensation," and the seeing, or being aware of blue, also called a "sensation." A tree, as seen, is called "perception," and the seeing of the tree called a "perception" too. From this grand ambiguity trouble has arisen continually. The strife between "interactionism" and "parallelism": the conception of thought and consciousness as stuff or things, and conversely, the conception of perceived objects as figments of "mind:" are only details of the results, of this confusion.

A radical reform in terminology has been well started, with excellent results. The term *consciousness,* in scientific psychology, is used to designate *awareness.* It is distinctly *not* used to indicate the objects, or contents, of which one is aware. Colors, sounds, odors, are not consciousness: they are *contents, data,* or *objects* of consciousness. The awareness of these colors, sounds, or odors, or of anything else, is consciousness.

The term "sensation" is apparently lost to scientific usage. No agreement can be secured to use it in one only of its three most frequent meanings, and hence is is impossible to tell in current usage when it means (1) sense-data, (2) consciousness (awareness) of sense-data, and (3) the physiological process conditioning the awareness of sense data. The term is best avoided altogether at present. "Perception" and "thought" we may still hope to salvage, and use them as meaning either two sorts of awareness, or awareness under two sorts of conditions. We shall herein use the terms in this way, and never as indicating contents or objects of awareness.

In the case of the terms "feeling" and "emotion," on the other hand, the emphasis on the content has become so pronounced that we may safely employ them to mean content only, never using them for the awareness which we may have of such contents. The feeling (or emotion) of fear, for example, is an object, or objective process of which one may be aware: the awareness of fear is consciousness of fear, but is not fear itself.

We may now return to the first point of method mentioned above, namely, the empirical basis from which scientific psychology starts, and with which it must constantly keep in touch. It may be said of physical science that it starts from observed facts: but this statement is not sufficiently broad to express the empirical basis of psychology. For psychology, the facts may be summed up in the statement that *we are aware of certain things.* We must consider, therefore, in psychology, not only the *observed things,* but also the *observing,* or *being aware of* these things, and the *we* who observe them. Neglect of any of these factors is a fault of arbitrary selection: an ignoring of part of the empirically given situation: which vitiates the method from the start and prevents it from becoming really psychological. For psychology is just the study of experience as it occurs, or it is nothing: and to ignore what is given in the experience is to abandon the first principle of science. Any "psychology" which ignores the fact of consciousness (awareness) is therefore a purely speculative exercise, or else is physical science in masquerade.

By the principles of parsimony (the avoidance of unnecessary hypotheses), we eliminate at the start the metaphysical theories of epistemological dualism which has played so pernicious a role in the history of the Anglo-German psychology. Experience does not give us directly two worlds of objects physical and mental. The fallacious conclusions in this regard have largely been due to the confusion of *awareness* and *content* under the one term of "mind" or "consciousness." Because the awareness of an object is not the object itself, and because the same term (consciousness) has been used to indicate at one time the object, at another time the awareness, the theory of two worlds—the world of mind (in the objective sense) and the world of physical realities—has been too easily adopted.* What we find at the start is not any

---

*This theory, which is the source of the traditional and fruitless controversy between "parallelism" and "interactionism"—with neither of which scientific psychology is in the least concerned—is due to Malebranche rather than to Descartes, and is set forth in the most crystal clearness in the former's *Entretiens sur la métaphysique* (which has unfortunately not been translated into English). From Malebranche the theory was taken over by Locks, who transmitted it to Hume. From Hume it passed over to the German psychology. By throwing off the shackles of this preposterous theory, psychology has grasped the chance of becoming scientific.

The account of consciousness given in this chapter might, on superficial examination, be branded as "interactionism:" but it is by no means that. The "interactionism" which has long been the bugaboo of the "parallelists" is a theory of causal relations between organic processes and contents of consciousness. The traditional arguments against this sort of "interactionism" are perfectly valid, although they do not in the least support the rival error of "parallelism" between the organic processes and contents of consciousness. Each of these schools has used the term "consciousness" and its cognates mainly to designate *awareness,* in stating their own theories: but has interpreted the other theory of the other school as if the term meant *content.*

The philosophical distinction between materialism and idealism has no importance for psychology because from the empirical point of view both amount to the same thing. The materialist believes in a world of "real matter," that is of imperceptible physical objects, upon which is superposed a world of perceptible or mental objects; the real objects acting upon his sense organs, and through them upon the general organism, produce in his mind the "sensation" or "idea" which is the sole object of his awareness, and which is, strictly speaking, a personal possession of his, being "in his

such bifurcation of objectivity into an observable world of mental objects and a world (supposedly observable) of physical objects, but merely a world *of objects of which we are aware.* Any further construction must be a result of analysis and experimentation and not of presupposition. Thus, by being careful and critical at the start, we avoid the naive acceptance of a metaphysical theory which has been long our curse. By avoiding "metaphysics" in the sense of careful attention to details of experience, psychology has in the past become unfortunately "metaphysical" in the bad sense of the term: that is, in the sense of adopting without criticism unnecessary metaphysical speculations.

The principles so far laid down as fundamental to scientific psychology exclude at once the dangers of mysticism, and exclude with them the confusions which abound in psychoanalysis and in the "behaviorism" or physiologized psychology of certain radicals,* and paves the way for a genuine physi-

---

mind" for his sole benefit and not observable by any one else. The idealist, being a trifle more logical, but starting from the same dualistic basis, points out that the physical object, being imperceptible) is entirely removed from our knowledge and hence cannot even be assumed to exist, since we might just as logically assume behind the hypothetical "real physical world" another hypothetical "realer" world and behind that a "still more real" world, and so on *ad infinitum.* In other words it is foolish to make hypotheses about existence outside the world of experience. The idealist, however, retains the materialistic conception of the perceptible world, as a figment and personal possession of his mind, and this is the essential metaphysical position which renders both idealism and materialism incompatible with empirical psychology.

*See Singer: *Journal of Philosophy, Psychology, etc.,* 1911, Vol. 8, pp. 180-186; Watson: *Psychological Review,* 1913, Vol. 20, pp. 158-177.

ological psychology or psychobiology. The Freudian doctrine of an unconscious-consciousness, is
possible on no other basis than that of epistemological dualism. On this basis also develops "behaviorism" which is the attempt to find the physiological factors which parallel the mind (conceived
as a purely spiritual entity), in order to ignore the
mind from that point on and deal only with its correlate in the other realm. Behaviorism depends
on the theory of parallelism between "mind" and
"body," whereas Freudianism apparently proceeds on the basis of interactionism, although it
might possibly work as well on a parallelistic
assumption. On a strictly psychobiological basis,
empirically laid, neither of these arbitrary systems
can be developed. Consciousness as actual
awareness: objects of consciousness treated as objects and not as awareness; leave nothing for
further consideration except the biological processes with which the consciousness is actually or-
ganized, and the stimuli as physical concepts. Consciousness which is not consciousness is not empirically found: and since consciousness is not a
thing, when it ceases to be consciousness it ceases
to exist.

The mystical concept of the "unconscious" is
impossible as a derivative from immediate experience. Awareness either is awareness or is nothing. A concept of awareness which at the same

time is not awareness, is impossible if we avoid the fallacy of the ambiguous middle term. As concerns the content of consciousness (which seems to a large extent to be what the proponents of the unconscious mean by their use of the term "consciousness") many contents of which we cease to be aware may still exist as physical objects, but not as content. The sound which comes through my open window, but which I no longer hear after I close the window, is no longer content of my consciousness: it is no longer something of which I am aware although, for all I am able to prove, it may still exist or continue as a sound. If it exists it is "in the unconscious" only in the literal sense of the term, in which anything existing of which I am not aware may be said to be in the unconscious realm.

As concerns thought or ideation, the situation is the same empirically as that concerning perception. If I am not thinking of something, that is, if I have no thought-awareness of it, I am unconscious of it. There are many things in Africa, doubtless, of which I am unconscious. Doubtless also, there are things of which I once was conscious but of which I am conscious no longer. Conscious-unconsciousness however, whether as perception or thought, is something for which there is no factual evidence. If we, on the other hand, take the term "consciousness" in the older sense of *content*, the same thing holds true as holds in perception. The things in Africa or the things of which I thought yesterday may exist, or they may not exist today. If I am not thinking of them, or perceiving them, they certainly are "in the unconscious" (if they exist at all) in exactly the same sense as that in which the whole universe or those major parts of it of which I do not happen to be conscious, are "in my unconscious."

The Freudian doctrine of consciousness as a *stuff* which, after it has functioned, is stored away somewhere like the printer's type which is returned to its case after being used, has no more empirical basis than has an exactly corresponding conception of finger movements which, after having occurred, are somewhere stored up as motionless movements. Just as the movement exists only during the motion, so consciousness exists only while one is conscious: and just as the original occurrence of the movement leaves biological structures so modified that the movement may occur again, so consciousness occurring once, leaves the biological mechanism so modified that it may recur.*

---

*In rejecting the theory of the unconscious mind, we do not necessarily deny the existence of consciousness of low degree, so low that it is with difficulty made a basis for reproductive imagination (memory), although it may involve a modification of the neural mechanism, and so may have an effect on further consciousness and action. In fact, we must admit the occurrence of consciousness in a scale of degrees ranging from the higher, which we call *attentive,* to the very low. These low degrees of consciousness, however, are not really *subliminal,* but merely *near* liminal. They are low, or obscure, *at the moments of their* occurrences. This conception of low-degree consciousness is by no means the equivalent of the Freudian con-

It may be claimed that unconscious mental processes occur without our being aware of them. This is verbal quibbling, with a vengeance. The consciousness of which we are speaking, is awareness: we are, so far, not concerned with any sort of mental processes than those in which consciousness occurs. In no case do we say that we are aware of the awareness: awareness is always awareness of something else. To say that we are aware of something, and at the same time not aware of it, is quite meaningless.

The ambiguity of the term "consciousness" is undoubtedly a factor contributing to the Freudian confusion over the "unconscious." "Consciousness" (content) may exist, of which one is not "conscious" (aware.) The use of the same term for the two different things makes it easy for the confused pseudo-psychologist to believe that consciousness may be unconscious, in some profound sense. But this verbal confusion although a great help to the theory of "unconscious mind" is not its vital source.

Sweeping aside the terminological confusion in

---

ception of unconscious mind, and it cannot be substituted for the latter without the destruction of the psychoanalytic system.

We are moreover not arguing against the possibility of real cases of "divided personality," to certain details of which Morton Prince has applied the term *co-conscious*. These cases must be examined, clinically, experimentally, and analytically, unprejudiced by Freudian or other theories of unconsciousness, and in the full light of the facts of integration, retention, and recall. Psychologists are not yet ready to make final conclusions concerning the mechanisms involved in these cases, and there is little use in dragging them into the present discussion. We may for the moment ignore their problems, as the Freudians have done.

which the believer in "unconscious mental processes" commonly lurks, he might state his claim
as follows: In addition to mental processes, *i.e.*,
organic processes involving consciousness (awareness), there are other processes, which while they
do not involve awareness, involve something which
is more than mere physiological process: something resembling consciousness, but not conscious.
This "unconscious mental" factor is therefore an
x, an unknown, and can not be pointed out in any
definite experience. Such an hypothesis might be
made. One might also hypothesize a *y* factor, a *z*
factor, and an infinity of other factors, all equally
unknown, equally beyond experience. But science
does not indulge in the positing of hypothetical
entities whose only qualification is that, they being
unknown, we can not know that they do not exist.
Hypotheses which are by their nature removed
from any possibility of verification, are never constructed in science.

A study of the function of the biological mechanism entirely aside from the consciousness which
we empirically find bound up with it, is entirely possible: this is what is generally known as *physiology,*
Physiology as such leaves room for the study of
the specific mechanism associated with consciousness and of the nature of the association: this is
what is actually included in psychology. Psychology since the time of Aristotle has, as a matter of

fact, been largely a study of behavior, that is to say, the conscious reactions of the organism; the modern system which calls itself "behaviorism" differs from psychology only in that it arbitrarily limits its methods of observation, and in that it is unable to explain why it studies these conscious reactions as it does, instead of studying general physiology.

The ecstatic knowledge of the philosophical mystics might be included in the scheme of psychology if it were empirically demonstrated. Since, however, neither the objects known, nor the knowing, can be analyzed; and since the alleged ecstasy can be readily interpreted, on the basis of empirical facts, as an emotional experience pure and simple, scientific psychology excludes it on the principle of parsimony. One hypothesis, namely: consciousness in two forms, as *perception* (including both sense-perception and the perception of relations) and as *thought;* includes all empirical facts, not merely those of common-place experience but also the alleged ecstasy of the mystics. Hence scientific psychology must be, as it has been since Aristotle, inflexibly hostile to and exclusive of mysticism.

The tender-mindedness which leads to short cuts and ambiguous middle terms is sternly repressed by scientific method. The most arduous road and the longest is preferred to the short and easy cut where the longest alone conforms to the maxims of scientific method. The anecdotal argument and the historical method in general give place to carefully deduced working hypotheses and experimental verification. Nothing is needed to continue the progress which psychology has been making for two thousand years except scrupulous attention to the principles of scientific method.

By the law of parsimony the working hypotheses in regard to action of the overt physiological sort are the working hypotheses for perception-reactions, thought-reaction, and emotional reactions.* One set of laws for heredity, whether mental or physical; one set of laws for instinct, whether unconscious or conscious; one set of laws for habit formation, whether for habits of doing or habits of perceiving, or habits of thinking or habits of feeling: that is the requirement, except in so far as the rigid generalization of empirical facts may demand the addition of supplementary hypotheses.

The philosopher's generalization against innate ideas therefore falls to pieces in scientific psychology. Habits of doing—walking, visual coordina-

---

*This rapprochement of biology and psychology has not been possible until the recent development of scientific psychology. Ten years ago psychology had absolutely no biological foundation, although it was strongly felt that such foundations must be discoverable. No fundamental use of biological facts was made in psychology (although biological data and biological theories were frequently mixed with the psychological materials in text books); and I felt constrained to minimize the value of biology to the psychologist. (*System of Psychology, 1910, p. 8.*) This was the proper attitude at the time; but the Reaction Arc Hypothesis has changed the situation. We can now make full use of biological principles and facts, and biology becomes the indispensable foundation of psychology.

tion, etc.—are given to the human animal through the laws of heredity in a partially completed stage: not built up entirely through experience in the history of the individual. There is every reason to assume, therefore, that habits of thinking, habits of emotional reaction, and habits of perception, in a more or less developed form occur in the same way. Biologically, innate ideas as well as innate emotions, are entirely probable. Further analysis must show the exact stage of completeness in which these arise. The assumption of their being learned in their entirety is without foundation. However space perception might be built up in the case of an animal which began its experience with nothing but materials out of which such perception could be developed, it is quite improbable that the human animal has to build it up in such a way. It is not impossible that the infant in its first search for the nipples of its mother has a conscious desire for food, or for the nipple: neither is it improbable that the bird, itself perhaps hatched in an incubator and having never seen a nest, has an idea of the nest which it builds before it has commenced building. Assumption to the contrary is arbitrary and neglects the known facts of heredity.

Scientific psychology cannot assume, as is frequently done by superficial psychology, that instinctive actions are necessarily nonvolitional, or that the preconception of the end to be attained by the action is not involved in instinctive acts. Observation supports our position on the first point: one of the most impressive of the "instincts"—the sexual—is unquestionably strongly volitional in many of its unlearned details. The boy who, at a certain age begins to "take interest in girls" in the various little ways which mark the arousal of the sex instinct, is by no means acting in an involuntary way: a part of his instinctive activity is the strong desire and will to act in that way: a way which perhaps earlier he scorned and ridiculed.

In the formation of habits, the same principle of integration which is required to explain the modification of a reaction such as occurred in Pavlov's dogs, where the substitution of a sound for smell or taste as the stimulation for the flow of saliva is brought about, is sufficient to explain the *association of ideas* and the *development of perception.* This principle is so central to scientific psychology that it is useful to present it in some detail here.

The Biological Conditions of Consciousness

The function of every nerve cell with the important exception of one class (receptors), is of precisely the same kind as the function of every other nerve cell in the body, viz.: *to be irritated or stimulated, and to irritate in turn another cell.* This is a statement which sums up the situation as far as present observations go.

The nerve cell may receive the stimulation (1) from a primary source: it may be irritated by light, or air vibration, or pressure (as on the skin), or by chemicals, such as sugar or citric acid. In these cases, where the source of the irritation is a physical stimulus, the nerve cell is called a *receptor.**

Or (2), the cell may be irritated by another neuron. Thus, the receptor, having been irritated by a physical stimulus irritates in turn a nerve cell in contact with it, and this second cell in turn irritates a third.

The irritation, conversely, may be passed on either (1) to another nerve cell, or (2) to muscle or gland cells. The irritation of these *effectors,* as muscle and gland cells are called, is the ultimate object of the process, and these effectors perform, in contraction or secretion, the work which adjusts the animal body as a whole, to the environment which supplies the stimuli.

Nerve cells differ importantly from each other in size: in the energy with which they "discharge" (stimulate other cells), and in the details of their local arrangement. These differences are structural, and influence the function of groups of the cells taken together.

A possible exception to the similarity of function

---

*While the statement is made for nerve cells only, it applies also to certain epithelial cells which have the nerve-cell function. Only in the class of receptors are such quasi-neural epithelial cells found and only in a few senses: certainly in the auditory and gustatory.

is in the fact that certain nerve cells *may* have the power of functioning intermittently when continuously stimulated. The ganglion cells of the heart, and those which discharge to the muscles of respiration, are supposed to have this peculiarity. This is a matter which is at present not important for our purposes, although highly important for general physiology. It, however, should not be lost sight of since it may prove of unforseen importance.

In the absence of specific proof therefore, we must abandon the phrenological hypothesis which has ruled neural physiology until lately: the hypothesis that consciousness is dependent on the specialized functions of certain groups of neurons set apart from the other sorts of neurons. Not only is proof of such specialization lacking, but the hypothesis is quite unnecessary. The evidence which has formerly been accepted is now clearly seen to be a misinterpretation of the facts*: and the *reaction-arc-hypothesis*** is not only a perfect substitute for the older phrenological assumption so far as that was applied, but has an extension of

---

*Reference is here to the abolition of certain functions by the pathological affection of certain brain areas in man, and by operations experimentally performed on animals. These affections and operations interrupt the reaction-arcs, making certain previously fixed reactions impossible; and hence produce corresponding defects in consciousness.

**This has been known as the *reflex-arc* hypothesis, but the old name is confusing, and in view of the transformation made by scientific psychology in the old form of the hypothesis, it is better to rename it. The term *reflex* is thereby allowed to carry its more customary meaning of non-conscious, or physiological, reaction.

application very much wider than the former, clearing up important points the former left unexplained; and hence, by the principles of parsimony, it must be adopted.

Mechanically, the function of the nervous system is the production of *responses*: that is: the action of effectors in specific ways, consequent upon specific action of receptors. The central nervous system (which includes the ''autonomic'' system, which in turn includes the ''sympathetic'' system) is hence to be regarded as an enormously complicated switchboard, connecting the receptors with the effectors in an intricate way, *and is to be regarded as nothing else.*

Certain definite responses, or *reactions* of the organism, are accompanied by, or involve, consciousness. A sudden loud sound produces both a *start,* by contraction of striped muscle (and usually of smooth muscle also), and certain recognizable effects on glands; and it also produces *consciousness* of the sound, and indirectly consciousness of ''startle.''* A spoken word falling upon the ear may produce a vocal response—action of the muscles of the throat and face—also awareness of the word or its meaning.

From these facts, the construction of the re-

---

*This ''startle'' is not necessarily *fear:* a great deal of bad psychology, especially ''child psychology,'' has resulted from the confusion of startle and fear.

action-arc hypothesis is inevitable. Consciousness (awareness) is the result of, or the accompaniment of, or a part of (the phrasing is for the present immaterial) certain reactions involving the activity of a complete arc from receptors to effectors.

Certain stimulations which obviously produce afferent current: *i.e.,* the action of receptors, and of chains of neurons leading to the brain, also produce consciousness although the complete reaction may not be easily identifiable. The stimulation of the visual receptors by printed words; or of the ear by spoken words, produces consciousness of the words or of their meaning, although no specific activity of gland or muscle as a result of the neural process, may be noticeable. Certain actions also are accompanied by consciousness, although no definite afferent current may be readily assignable as the source of the efferent current producing the act. The thought of some one approaching may be combined with the lifting of the head and eyes: the determination to play tennis may be combined with the closing of a book and the stretching out of the hand to grasp the racquet. In all these cases, which at first blush seem to be exceptions to the reaction-arc principle it can be shown that the hypothesis is fully borne out.

It is not necessary to assume that all reactions involve consciousness: but only that all consciousness depends on reaction. This hypothesis is guar-

anteed by the law of parsimony, in that it involves
the least possible extension of the general hypothesis of the nervous system as a mechanism for response: and as we shall see it includes without
farther extension than can be made empirically, the
large mass of known details concerning the mental
life.

So far as the empirical evidence goes, it is altogether in favor of the reaction-arc hypothesis.
Perception, at least, is impossible if the arc is interrupted. In the case of vision, experiments on
animals, and human clinical cases, make this point
clear. Destroying the retinae; cutting the optic
nerves; cutting the optic tract behind the brain-
stem; destroying the occipital lobes (of the cerebral hemispheres) to which the optic tracts lead;
or cutting the connections between the occipital
lobes and the remainder of the cerebral hemispheres; produce the one and the same results—
blindness—by interrupting the arcs from the visual
receptors to the effector systems, and destroying
the possibility of a visual reaction. There is no
single system of efferent channels from the hemispheres which the visual reaction need follow:
hence, to block completely the visual reactions by
operation on the efferent side of the arc, all the
efferent channels from the hemispheres would have
to be cut. This would cut off the possibility of not
only visual, but all reactions—and the patient
would not survive.

Assuming that perception depends primarily on reactions which begin in special sense receptors, pass through the central nervous system to effectors; and terminate in the activity of these receptors; we still have to provide for the other form of consciousness, namely, *thought* or *thinking*. It has long been assumed that thought has "motor power:" that activity is produced by thought but this, according to our conception now, is a putting of the cart before the horse. Really, thought is dependent on, or a part of, a reaction: but where is the reaction initiated? Not in the cerebrum, for it has been demonstrated that there are no receptors there: and not, primarily at least, in any other part of the brain. For reasons which will be explained shortly, the thought-reactions—that is, the complete reactions on which thought is dependent, or which include or involve thought—must be assumed in most cases to be initiated in the receptors in the *muscle spindles,* in the striped muscles of the trunk, limbs, face, and vocal organs.

Thought, therefore, not only may lead to motor activity: it is, in its primary phase* initiated by muscular activity.

The form of consciousness which is sometimes set as a third kind over against perception and thought, viz., emotional consciousness, is really

---

*The reservation "in its primary phase" will be explained later.

perceptual, and is already provided for by the well known theory of Lange.*

An emotion, or a feeling, is exactly a bodily condition: a real physical fact: which is perceived through the receptors in the viscera (and to a certain extent in the soma also) in the same way as that in which color is perceived through the receptors in the retina, or sound through the receptors in the cochlea of the ear. Put in terms of the reaction hypothesis, we say that the emotional reactions are initiated by receptors lying in the viscera (and in the soma) and that the reactions terminate in as wide a range of activities as do perceptual reactions generally.

The application of the reaction hypothesis to emotions is frequently confusing to one unfamiliar with it: and in fact to many who suppose that they are familiar with it, but really fail to grasp the essential point. Careful following of the scheme

---

*Unfortunately, the "James-Lange" theory of the emotions, as it is called usually, is most frequently stated in James' terms, in which it is a compromise between the scientific view of Lange, and old-fashioned dualism. The formulation of Lange is here followed. Although James in America, Lange in Denmark, and Sutherland in Australia developed almost simultaneously theories of the emotions which have remarkable resemblances (all three derived from Darwin's *Expression of the Emotions in Man and Animals,* as the authors admit), the three theories are not actually equivalent, and hence the scientific view should be referred to as the "Lange" theory rather than the "James-Lange" or "James-Lange-Sutherland" theory. To James however belongs the substantial credit of having gained the attention of the scientific world to the common feature of the theories.

Mosso's theory (see Appendix, to Goddard's *Psychology*) is merely a statement of Lange's theory in terms of the divisions of the nervous system. Unfortunately, few psychologists or physiologists have ever read Lange's presentation: the majority have taken James' presentation both of his own and of Lange's views.

here given, drawing a diagram if necessary, will however make it clear.

Suppose that as you are writing at your desk, a stray bullet passes just above your hand, smashing the pen from your grasp, and buries itself in the wall. The stimulation of visual, tactual, and auditory receptors starts activity over a number of reaction circuits. These currents enter, some the spinal cord, some the brain stem: pass upward to the cerebrum, are switched from point to point therein, and finally are led back to the brain stem, from which some routes pass directly, some by way of the cord, to the muscles of the trunk, limbs, face and throat: to the smooth muscles of the viscera and to the glands. Dependent on this very complicated reaction (or involved in it) is the *perception* of the passage of the bullet and its attendant damage. If the nervous action stopped at this point, there would be no consciousness of emotion, although there would be a real emotion set up: for the changes in glands and muscles (chiefly the visceral changes) *are* the emotion. If the reaction described were all, there would be an *emotion not experienced*.

There is however a second reaction immediately. The changes in the striped muscles excite receptors in the muscle spindles. The changes in smooth muscles excite receptors in adjacent connective and epithelial tissues. A little later, the altered secretions of the glands may begin to excite receptors in various tissues.

From the complex excitation of these receptors the second reaction, which may be rather long drawn out, is initiated. Current over these new arcs flows into the cord, and brain stem; and from these points upward to the hemispheres: from the hemispheres the flow is outward again to produce new muscular and glandular disturbances, or to increase or inhibit those already started. And this second reaction produces (or involves) the consciousness (or awareness) of the emotion, which would otherwise remain a mere non-mental fact, like light unseen or sound unheard.

The Simple Viewpoint of Scientific Psychology

Enough has been said to make it clear that Scientific Psychology is a far simpler and clearer subject than the earlier system on which Freudianism, Christian Science, and Behaviorism are based. It no longer assumes a world of "mental facts" requiring study apart from the real world. It no longer deals in "sensations" and "images" and "thoughts" as analysable components in a "stream of consciousness." Scientific Psychology accepts the fact of a real world external to the organism, and of an *I*, connected with the organism, which can be aware of both the real world outside, and

also of the organism. Consciousness ceases to be
a mystic stuff, and is just the *awareness* of anything. No longer do we assume an elementary
form of mental stuff called "sensation," and develop a cumbrous theory of "perception" as a
mental elaboration of the sensation stuff. The
term "perception" is retained for the primary
form of awareness, and this is seen to have a scale
of complexity which follows the general laws of
habit formation. The term "sensation," if used
at all, becomes a general name for the perceptual
process when considered from the point of view of
the *receptors*: in which condition it really has a
much more definite meaning than in the older system, in which it stood in a confused way for sense
object, for consciousness, and for nervous process.*
Thought becomes the term for awareness or consciousness of objects not actually stimulating the
special sense organs through which they were primarily perceived, and "image" becomes the name
of objects thought-of: not a special kind of object,
but an object of which one is conscious in a special
way. It would be better perhaps, on account of
the misleading associations of the term "image,"
and "sensation," not to use them at all in scientific psychology.

---

*Some time earlier, the author attempted to use "sensation" systematically
in one of its three common meanings, viz., for the sense object: such as
color or sound. But this attempt was not successful, since the other meanings are clung to by readers. It is far simpler and accurate to use the terms
sense-data or *sentienda* for these outer facts.

All these changes, flowing from the illuminating concept of reaction, vastly simplify the field of psychology, which every beginner in the study has found to be one of harrowing confusion. The view of Scientific Psychology is after all the "common sense" view which every one takes when he is not laboring under the obsession which philosophers, physicists, and psychologists have for so long been building up: and shuts off the stream of mystical construction which has so seriously delayed progress. Nevertheless, it is not a complete break with the history of psychology, but a real development, which puts psychology in its direct line of advancement after the long detour through Malebranche, Locke, and Wundt. Having closer affinity in principle with Aristotle than with the Anglo-German School, it makes use of all the empirical accomplishments of modern psychologists and physiologists.

The Development of Perception

The various conscious reactions (perceptual, including emotional: and ideational) are in part provided for by heredity and natural development— that is, are instinctive— and are in part learned. The general laws of habit-formation cover the development of perception and of thought, and the modification of emotion. The instinctive reactions receive further development through experience;

and conversely, all learning is based on instinctive material. Specific types of habits, whether conscious habits or "merely physiological" habits, will follow specific rules, but these minor principles must be discovered, not assumed before investigation.

We do not know at what stage of development the child's perceptions commence. It is hardly possible that the world is a "buzzing, blooming confusion" to him, since there is evident a certain degree of organization of reaction from the moment of birth. But just what degree of organization of conscious reaction is instinctively present we cannot yet determine—and the speculations of the experts in child study have little force. We do know, however, that whatever the starting point, the development must follow a certain scheme, ascertained by scientific analysis and experiment, and we can trace this scheme back to a point which is, in all probability, much lower than the actual stage of development of the infant at birth. This scheme is illustrated by certain experiments on dogs: although it might be as clearly made out from observations on human individuals.

If a dog, fasting long enough so that he will eat eagerly, is shown his customary food, or allowed to smell it, his saliva will commence to flow. If, at a time when no food is present, a bell is rung, there will ordinarily be little, if any, effect on the salivary secretion, although pricking up of the ears, or some similar action, may occur. If the dog, before being fed, is shown (or allowed to smell) food, and at the same time the bell is rung: and if this procedure is repeated on a number of successive days, an "association" between the two reactions will be set up: that is, the arcs will become connected in the cerebrum, so that the ringing of the bell will produce the flow of saliva, without the food stimulus being required.*

Obviously, the two reaction-arcs which were at first somewhat independent: the arc from the olfactory receptors (assuming the food to have been smelled, and not seen) to the salivary glands, and the arc from the auditory receptors to (let us say) the ear muscles: have become connected in the cerebrum so that the current flowing in over the afferent part of the one, may now flow out over the efferent part of the other: or, as we say, one discharge may be *drained into* the other.

This particular aspect of integration which we generalize as *drainage,* and which is experimentally verified, we find will apply to and explain all habit

---

*In the same way, it should be possible to demonstate the production of the usual effects of the bell by the food stimulus: this is, however, not so simple, the arc from the bell stimulus to the salivary reaction being more easily established than the arc from the food stimulus to the other reaction. It will be found in general that the more invariable reaction will more easily "drain" the current from another stimulus into its efferent channel, than will the more variable reaction drain the current from the other stimulus into its efferent channel. The food-saliva reaction is much more fixed prior to the experiment, than is the reaction to the bell, which may take one of several forms: and that invariability is just a strong tendency to discharge through definite efferent channels.

formation, including both the development of perception, and the association of ideas.

Let us suppose that the visual presentation of an orange, to a child of a certain age, is merely color. The consciousness of the color depends on the activity of a certain reaction arc which we will call V—v: V being the receptor activity, and v the terminal effector activity. Let us suppose that the child smells the orange peel also, is allowed to taste the juice, and grasp the orange in his hand. We may represent the olfactory reaction by O—o, the gustatory by G—g, the tactual by T—t.

If two or more of these reactions occur simultaneously, or in immediate succession, and this is repeated, so that eventually each reaction has occurred a sufficient number of times with each of the others, we will have the conditions established for integration of the same sort as that occurring in the experiment on the dog described above. The several reaction circuits become connected (in the cerebrum) so that the afferent current from any of the four senses represented may flow out over any of the original efferent routes. In other words, stimulations of one sense, as for example vision, may produce the effects formerly produced by stimulation of one of the other senses: or may produce, in a measure, the effects of all. The child eventually, from the visual stimulation alone, perceives, not color merely, but the orange, as a round, yellow, odorous, heavy body with sweet juice.

Manifestly, the development of perception is more complicated than the scheme here presented, because other perceptions are also being formed, and they mutually modify each other. With the consolidation (integration) of the reaction-arcs also goes modification of the terminal muscular activities: and in many cases these activities, at first movements of the whole body, become modified into *words*—standardized reactions of the complex system of vocal muscles. The illustration given above is nevertheless typical, in spite of its simplification.

The actual development of perception does not follow the course psychology has traditionally assigned it, and which is described by nearly all the text-books with great fidelity to the tradition, as the addition of "imagination" to "sensation," (assuming that "sensation" means here the simplest form of perception.) Imagination is not essentially included in the process just described, nor does the concept of associative reproduction fit the case. The development of perception may proceed in independence of imagination, although it is a basis for the development of the latter. It is possible that perceptual habits may be modified by thought-activity (imagination) occurring subsequently, but even this does not mean that in later perceptions imagination will participate.

The Association of Ideas

One of the most conspicuous characteristics of thought, and one about which a great deal of information has been accumulated by empirical psychology, is the *association* of thoughts or "ideas."*

Ideas which have occurred in succession become enchained, so that the future occurrence of one brings about the reappearance of the others. Such associations may indeed be formed without the previous juxtaposition of the ideas, if the perceptions from which the ideas are drawn have occurred in close succession: this is in fact one of the most important methods of associating ideas. Thinking of several things in succession tends to establish the habit of thinking them in succession: and perceiving several things in succession also tends to establish the habit of thinking them in succession. The explanation of the association-habit is furnished by the reaction hypothesis, and at the same time the nature of the reaction-arc peculiar to thought-consciousness is clearly indicated by the associative peculiarities of thought.†

The association of ideas, is, from its description,

---

*Idea here is used in the sense of *being aware of something in the nonperceptual* way: it does not involve the notion of a different sort of *content* of the consciousness.

†The following account of the association of ideas, with the indication of the spindle receptors as the starting place of the associative thought reactions although so simple when stated that it seems improbable that it should not have been discovered long ago, was, I believe, first presented by me in the *Johns Hopkins Circular*, of March, 1914, in a paper on *Images and Ideas*. The theory of the development of perception given above was also sketched first in that paper.

manifestly a species of habit-formation and should conform to its general laws. Conversely, the known laws of the association of ideas should be applicable to habit formation in general, with such reservations as may be empirically found: differences in detail being expected when we pass from one type of habit to another, even if both are in the "mental" group, or both in the "motor" group.

If ideas are dependent on reactions, and if ideas are capable of association, it must be that the ideational reaction-arcs are of such a nature that the completion of one reaction may initiate another. Since reaction arcs terminate in muscles and in glands, it must be that in one of these tissues lie the neccessary receptors of the thought-arcs. The receptors in glands are as yet conjectural, and the glandular response is not of such nature that we could assume it to be the stimulus of reactions as prompt, as manifold, and as finely graded as thought-reactions apparently are. The striped muscles, however, are provided with a plentitude of receptors in the "muscle spindles," and the muscular responses are quick, finely graded, and of great complexity, competent to initiate reactions of an endless variety. The muscle-receptors are, therefore, in all probability, the beginnings of the thought-arcs:

If we assume the muscular initiation of thought-reactions, the mechanism of the association of ideas is at once clear, and it is also identified as the mechanism of habit-formation of a much wider range. Whenever a series of reactions is knit together so that eventually the series repeats itself if given the proper start, the muscle contractions are primarily the connecting links, each set of contractions being the terminus of one reaction and the stimulus for the next. The association of ideas is just one instance of this general type of habit-formation.

Suppose we represent three successive stimuli of special sense organs by A, B, and C. Let the receptor-processes resulting from these stimulations be A', B', and C', and the ultimate muscular activity of the reactions beginning in these receptor activities be a, b, and c.

The contraction a will then be the stimulus of a new process, a', in the spindle-receptors of the muscles affected: and this process, a' will be the beginning of a new reaction a'—x, which will become integrated in the cerebrum with the reaction $B'-b$, so that (following the scheme exemplified in the experiments of the dogs) the afferent current from a' tends to be "drained" into the efferent current to b. The contraction b, in turn, by its stimulation of spindle receptors, initiates a new reaction $b'-y$ in receptor action b', which tends to be drained into the next perceptual reaction, to c. If this series of reactions is repeated a number of times, the series of arcs *a'-b, b'-c,* and so on, is established, so that the perceptual stimulus *A* will cause the series of reactions *a, b, c,* and so on, without the need of the stimuli *B, C,* and so on. In other words, the *ideas* corresponding to the perceptions of *A, B, C,* and so on, have become *associated.*

Two illustrations of the serial connections of reactions will serve to make the mechanism clear: learning to waltz, and learning or "memorizing" a list of words. In the first case a "motor" habit is being formed: in the latter, a thought-habit, or association of ideas, is ultimately established. Neither process is really simple, since it starts from a complex of habits already formed, and the stimulations which operate in the formation of the habits are also complicated, but we may legitimately conclude that the contributory habits already in existence were formed in the same way as those under consideration. An attempt to start from conditions really simpler: that is, in infancy, is fallacious because we can interpret the learning of the infant only on the basis of the examination of the better known conditions of the adult.

The first reaction in waltzing, for the man, concludes in drawing the left foot straight back: the second, in drawing the right foot back and to the right: the third in moving the left foot laterally over to the right: the fourth in advancing the right foot straight forward: the fifth in advancing the left foot diagonally to the left: and the sixth, in moving the right foot laterally over to the left.* At this point the series commences again, and may be kept up without change for a certain length of time, then, by moving the right foot backwards instead of forwards on a fourth step, the series is *reversed,* this step forming the first in a new series in which the right foot goes back at *one* and the left forward at *four.* The series must also be modified as the steps are taken, by turning, so that the absolute direction of forward and back are continually changing: and the relative directions and lengths of the steps must be modified in accordance with the needs of the floor and the activities of other dancers: but the first thing which has to be done, if waltzing is to be learned quickly and effectively, is to form the two series (direct and reverse) of six steps each, and make the series mechanically perfect.

In learning the waltz steps, each step is first initiated separately, as the result of an elaborate system of thought and perceptual reflexes. A trained waltzer, however, initiates only the first step, and if the floor is ample and progress unimpeded he may for some time thereafter give his attention to conversation with his partner, the

---

*The details given are for the old or "standard" waltz, not the at present more popular "skip" waltz, in which as in the "twostep" the feet are brought together by the second step, and again separated by the third.

series of steps taking care of itself. The stages in the progression of this habit are material for analysis.

The stimuli, in the several cases, we may suppose to be the words "left," "right," and "over," addressed to the pupil's auditory receptors; or may be significant movements of the instructor's hands, affecting the visual receptors: or tactual stimuli applied by the instructor's hands, or combinations of these. Each stimulus, or group of stimuli, produces a movement; and each movement in turn produces a new set of stimuli, initiating a discharge which, if allowed to follow its normal course, would be a reaction conditioning the consciousness of the particular leg movement, but which is actually drained outwards from the cerebral hemispheres into the next movement. In this way, the movements are connected by direct arcs, the consciousness connected with them becoming less and less vivid, through the elimination of the original efferent connections of the arcs from the muscles, and the lessening tendency of these arcs to dominate the nervous system: until finally there is practically no consciousness of the leg movement except at such times as the processes are interfered with.

Let us now consider the learning of the list of words, *coffee, brittle, quantity, aggravate, paper, sunny.* Suppose these words to be presented for learning either by sounds addressed to the auditory receptors, or by printed letter combinations addressed to the visual receptors. The perception of each of these words depends on a complicated reaction which we will suppose to have been already learned by the person who is to memorize the series: that is the words are already familiar as words, but the series has not yet been learned. Each word-stimulus, therefore, is the beginning of a reaction which will terminate in some muscular activity. This muscular activity will, in some cases be movements of the vocal muscles in speaking the words, and we may take this vocal activity as a type.

The speaking of the first word initiates, through its stimulation of receptors in the vocal muscles, a reaction process which is drained off into the reaction of speaking the second word. The speaking of the second word in turn initiates a reaction process which is drained off into the speaking of the third word, and so on. By sufficient repetition, the series is so linked together that the sight or sound of the first word will result in the accurate repetition of the whole list, although at no time during the learning need the words be vocalized to the extent of furnishing auditory stimuli.

The above is a very much simplified account of the formation of serial habits. The details of the interference and control of the process of reactions

of other sorts, and the mechanism by which the reactions are ultimately abbreviated or short cir-
cuited, are out of place here but have been treated
elsewhere. The complete muscular reaction is necessary during the learning process, but is largely
eliminated, in the interests of economy, after the
series have been thoroughly mechanized. Learning is obviously a process which has its own
abolition as its ideal, and it would be surprising
if we did not find the final mechanism of association characteristically different from that essential to the initiation of the learning process.

Integration and Attention

The essential features of the reaction hypothesis,
and the principle of "drainage" which is brought
in by the phenomena illustrated by the experiments
on the dogs, are generalized under the conception
of *integration*, which is the tendency of the central
nervous system to work as a whole, and not as a
collection of detached parts. This conception has
entered to replace the "phrenological" theory
above referred to, and the reaction hypothesis
properly takes its place as one phase of this general hypothesis.

The various reaction-arcs which are present at
one time *integrate* by becoming connected with each
other through the manifold synaptic system of the
cerebrum, so that they tend to form a single sys-

tem: a single great reaction arc, with multiple afferent routes and multiple efferent routes. In complete integration each receptor process is the starting point not only of the limited reaction process with which it is most uniformly connected (either through habit formation, or instinctive organization), but also in lesser degree of all the other reaction-arcs in operation at the time: and each terminal activity (muscular or glandular) is the result not only of a definite receptor process but of all the receptor processes which have immediately preceded it. In other words: every stimulation influences all the reactions of the organism, and every motor activity is determined by the total stimulation playing on the receptorial system. Integration probably is seldom perfect, but varies in degree from a high order to a minimum, the normal minimum being reached in dreamless sleep. This principle of integration has become the indispensable basal conception of psychobiology.

Empirical evidence, showing that all sorts of stimulations tend to affect not only the entire striped musculature; but also the smooth muscles of the blood vessels, of the digestive and genito-urinary system, and of the glands generally; and also the gland cells themselves; has been accumulated in considerable volume. The converse evidence that every activity is influenced by a wide range of stimulations in addition to the specific stimulation to which we normally ascribe it, is not so experimentally complete, but there is enough to establish the fact. Even such an apparently simple process as the movement of the finger in response to a sound, however well established by practice, shows marked variations according to the perceptual and ideational processes simultaneously in progress.

The consideration of the principle of integration explains fully the phenomenon which under the title of *attention* has so long puzzled the psychologists, and which, because of the former lack of explanation, has been treated as if it were a specific and detached mental function, in addition to the common facts of consciousness.

The more efficient an animal's reaction to a single source of stimulation, the more completely must its nervous system be integrated at the moment of reaction into a single system of reaction-arcs, in which the analytic arc from the receptors affected by the stimulation in question, to the most characteristic movements in the response, dominates the whole system. In the case of a man catching an approaching ball, for example, the specific visual process initiated by the ball-stimulus: a complex of effects on receptors in the retina and in the visual muscles: is the starting point of a unitary system of arcs terminating in the movements of the muscles of the arms and shoulders. But at the same time, the shouts of the crowd, the sight of the runner, the tactual and muscular processes in the trunk and limbs, are initiating a great number of other unitary arc systems. These various stimulations must not produce their characteristic reactions independently, or the main process will be disturbed: the afferent currents must be subordinated to the main line of discharge, so that they will assist it and not hinder it. At the same time, other muscular activities are necessary: attitudes of the legs and trunk must be assumed, but these cannot occur as independent movements: the efferent discharge to these effectors must be regulated by the main reaction to which they are necessarily auxiliary.

On the conscious side, the result of this integration is clear: the dominant consciousness is of the object stimulating the main reaction, and consciousness of other factors—the runner, the inequalities of the ground, and even the noise of the onlookers—although not excluded, is in subordination to the main object. This is the situation we commonly express by saying that the catcher's *attention* is on the ball, meaning that his most *vivid* consciousness is of the ball. In this case his sole consciousness is not of the ball, but the ball "occupies the focus" of attention, to use an old expression. Literally, there is *more* consciousness, or a higher degree of consciousness, of the ball.

The facts concerning attention, and its dependence on the degree of integration, furnish us with an interesting suggestion towards the solution of the problem of the relation of consciousness to neuromuscular action. We have found that consciousness depends, not on the action of individual neurons, but on the joint action, in a reaction-arc, *of a functionally related group of cells.* We see now that the more complex the system of cells acting together, the higher the degree of consciousness. These two details taken together suggest that mere reaction alone is not a sufficient condition for consciousness any more than mere neuron activity is. Some degree of absorption of the reaction (integration of the arc) into the total system of reactions is indicated as the lowest condition of consciousness, and complete dominance of the system as the possible upper limit. On this supposition it would be clear that the isolated knee-jerk, and kindred "physiological" reflexes could not be expected to be *conscious,* although attendant and consequent reactions may be conscious.

Poor attention; badly coordinated activities such as occur in stuttering; faulty circulatory adaptations (even digestive and respiratory processes must be integrated with the general reactive processes of the organism); and many sexual and nutritive insufficiencies, are defects of integration. The search for the origins and for means of cure of such conditions lies in part in the field of psychological research.

It is obviously a possibility that habits of integration—*habits of habits*—may be built up: and that a person's whole habit system may change, either gradually or quickly, producing, or rather being, a modification of personality. A man may have two or more integration systems which may alternate with each other according to circumstances, just as, on a smaller scale, he may have two language habits, French and English, one of which operates in given circumstances to the exclusion of the other. All these features of integration, together with the more striking cases in which personality changes with apparent abruptness and relative permanence so that the individual is not recognizable today except in anatomical feature, as the same man he was yesterday, demand thorough and patient examination on the basis of Scientific Psychology.

Application of the Reaction Hypothesis

The problem of the nature of the self and of personality is removed by Scientific Psychology from the realm of mysticism, and a beginning made in its understanding. Practically, a man's personality and character (the usages of the two terms are not at present clearly fixed) is his system of habits: and among these the emotional habits occupy a position of eminence. As experienced by the person, his "self" is largely his habitual emotional content: and the emotions, as we have seen above, are bodily functions which are perceived without analysis, but which, although unanalyzed consciously, are nevertheless physiologically definite. The relation of the self to functional disorders is therefore of especial interest.

Among the factors making up the self, desires are perhaps most consequential in the way of subsequent reactions of a "motor" sort (conduct or behavior in the usual meanings of the terms). Psychology has been culpably negligent in regard to the study of the desires, and the one positive service which the Freudians have done is in emphasizing the incompetence of our information (and also of their own information) on this important subject. We do not know whether there are fundamentally several desires, or only one kind of desire which arises in diverse circumstances. Desire is unquestionably a bodily process. Desire of food and desire of drink may have their seat in the alimentary canal: sex desires may have their seat in the special sex organs: desire of rest and desire of activity may be localized in the muscles. On the other hand, the seat of a desire (or of desire) may not be in the tissues which are most directly concerned in its production or its satisfaction. Information on these points is still to be acquired:

hence our knowledge of the principles of conduct is woefully inadequate, and Social Psychology is as yet in its swaddling clothes.

The reason for the statement that there is no place in Scientific Psychology for an "unconsciousness" of the Freudian type, or for an "unconscious" in any other than the literal significance of *not conscious at all,* should now be clear. Consciousness depends on a reaction: or, we may perhaps better say, it is a part of a total reaction. When the reaction is over, it no longer exists; and the consciousness connected with it is also non-existent. A habit may have been established, such that the reaction, and the consciousness, may re-occur at some future time. But just as the physiological part of the reaction is not something which can be laid away on a shelf after it occurs, so the consciousness is not a thing which can be preserved. To continue the existence of the consciousness over a period of weeks or days or even minutes, would necessitate the continuance of the reaction, and this we know does not occur.

Suppose I think of diving into a pool. The physiological reaction may be one of a large number: let us suppose it to be the saying of the words "dive into a pool." Suppose that next I turn my thoughts to mechanical subjects, and puzzle over the designing of a complicated piece of apparatus. Suppose that for twenty-four hours afterwards the pressing demands of a busy life keep my thoughts occupied with things other than pools and diving, until the sight of the same picture which first brought up the thought of diving brings it up again.

Where was the thought in the meantime? An unscientific psychology may answer: "In the unconscious mind:" but if we answer in non-mystical terms, we must say, "nowhere." The thought didn't exist at all in the intervening hours. To say that the thought continued its existence in any form, is to imply that the physiological reaction (the saying of the words) also continued in some form during the twenty-four hours during which in reality not only the muscles but the nervous system were fully occupied with other reactions (or asleep). Such an assumption it is plainly impossible to uphold in the face of empirical facts. That which really persisted, was an altered condition of the neurons: not a specific reaction or neural discharge, but an adjustment such that the discharge or the complete reaction may occur again on the proper stimulus.

Suppose again, that some habit of action, or tendency of thought, which was characteristic of my youth, reasserts itself after having been apparently absent from my life for many years. Where were the actions, where were the thought sequences, in the meantime? *They did not exist at all.* It is as foolish to suppose the persistence of the thoughts as it is to suppose the persistence of the actions. Modifications of the nervous system which were not completely effaced and which were at last permitted by the changing environment, or the growth or the decay of the nervous system, to influence reactions, completely suffice as explanation. The overruling principle of parsimony forbids us to raise a fantastic additional hypothesis where a hypothesis already in use supplies a full explanation.

All this, it may be urged, is a much ado about nothing. All the mystics mean is what is above expressed in our own terms: they have only expressed it in a different and metaphorical language. In a measure, this is true. The Freudians have added nothing to our knowledge of habit: they have merely restated familiar facts along with a great deal which is not fact, in the language of fairy tales. But the supposition that the restatement is unimportant is not correct. The Freudian statements do not mean to the psychoanalyst what our statements of fact mean to the scientist. And the supposition is emphatically refuted by the burgeoning of psychoanalysis upon the restatements. The whole poisonous vine, with its tendrils threatening to grasp and choke all forms of learning (to which threat we have referred on page 45) is rooted in the assumption of an "unconscious" which is not merely the nervous system, and not merely something which isn't conscious at all, but is truly a mystical *third kind of knowledge.*

For scientific psychology, every conscious process, like every act, has a causal basis. One is no more a matter of chance than is the other, and if it should be claimed that there is an element of unpredictability in the occurrence of ideas, it would necessarily have to be claimed also that there is an element of unpredictability in the action of the digestive system. Dreams, small incidents of every day life, no less than more important events, have causes, although the causes may not be understood by the person affected. And in every such case, the tracing down of the causes is a far more laborious work than is undertaken in the naive analogical "explanations" of the Freudian "Interpretation of Dreams" and "Psychopathology of Everyday Life." Psychology cannot be tender-minded: it cannot shrink from the harder task. The causes of mental and physiological activities alike are capable of being summed up in three groups: heredity: nurture and disintegrative changes in the neural mechanism: present environment (stimuli) and past experiences including conscious and non-conscious activities. Conscious activity in the past has its effects in both conscious and unconscious activity of the present, and non-conscious activity of the past may also have left an influence on conscious activity of the present. This is not a modern innovation or development, but has been the working basis of psychology for centuries.

It is evident that every science which deals with human activity, from philology to criminology and political geography, involves psychology. But psychology, when it is scientific, makes no attempt to abolish or absorb these sciences. Rather, it derives its material from them, and through the analytical and experimental study of these materials in the general light which it throws upon them attempts to make returns to the several sciences. That it has made small returns as yet, is, even if true, of small consequence. Of far greater consequence is the fact that it makes no false or misleading returns as does mystical psychology. Such returns as scientific psychology makes are best not made directly. No psychologist would attempt to conduct research in philology or in music. But philologists and musicians, having absorbed what psychologists have to offer, are unquestionably better equipped for their research than those more ignorant. Psychologists have in the past ten years or more made many important contributions to what is more accurately described as physiology than psychology, and must undoubtedly continue to do so for some years to come: but this is merely because too many physiologists have neglected to become familiar enough with psychological methods and technique to do adequate work in certain parts of their own field.

The most pressing application of psychology is in psychiatry. Psychiatry is at present a "medical" science, with little psychological foundation, although each psychiatrist has his private psychological theories—and bizarre enough some of them are, when the psychiatrist attempts, as he occasionally does, to impress them on others. Seldom is an eminent psychiatrist a good psychologist—although there are notable exceptions to this rule. So far, attempts to construct a system of psychology on the basis of unoriented observation of pathological details has been a necessary failure, and in Freud and his disciples the failure has been most impressive.

The development of a sound psychotherapeutics will certainly not be the work of the general psychologist. But when it is developed, it will be developed by psychopathologists of thorough training in scientific psychology. It cannot be developed by those who do not understand the requirements of scientific reasoning, or by those who do not know the empirical basis of mental science. A system which neglects the physical side of mind and substitutes mystical concepts is as futile as a purely physiological or behavioristic one. My present opinion is that the psychiatrist must always be paced by the physiological chemist, but must also be well instructed in psychology.

It is not, however, outside the province of the general psychologist to make suggestions of importance for the psychopathologist. One suggestion on the probable effects of prostitution and of abnormal sex experiences, a suggestion which cannot be ignored, I have already outlined above (page 110). The further discussion of the basis of habit and consciousness makes it possible to add thereto some important details.

The sex factor is, as has long been acknowledged, one of the determining factors in all conscious life. In the production of neuroses, it may perhaps be the most important factor of all. The effects of fear and worry, in connection with irregular sex relations, and the nervous shock of the pathological course of these relations, due to their furtiveness, cannot be neglected. These are some of the abnormalities of the sex life which have been obscured by a fog of theories, and upon which scientific psychology will surely throw light. But the role played by conscious acts, as over against ideas and emotional experiences which do not result in positive sex acts, is a question for examination. "Repression," in the common-sense interpretation of the term, seems to be a necessary feature of habit formation, and it has not been shown to have necessary evil consequences. The habit of not doing

is formed *by not doing*: and the complicated reactions of hesitation, vacillation, and "conflict"
of emotional ideas are, when prolonged, unquestionably detrimental to the integration of the nervous system. Useful activity (outward and ideational) is inhibited and interfered with so long as
the turmoil continues. Obviously, lines of conduct
which are not to be actualized, and the inducements
to them, should be excluded from the field of consideration as soon as possible, since the consideration thereof is precisely the disturbing complex
of reactions indicated. And the habit of not thinking of a certain thing, is best formed by *thinking
about something else*, just as the habit of not doing
a certain thing is formed by *doing something else*.

In a large number of neurotic cases, irregular
sex experiences as was earlier indicated, probably
play an important part in the history. Whether
the influence of these active experiences is
stronger than the influence of failure to suppress
desires without corresponding activity, no one can
at present say. In either case, there is danger of
beginning a division of personality. In the neurosis resulting from coitus with prostitutes the
division is actually commenced in the admission
of the emotional revulsion along with the sexual
desire and gratification. Most cases of pronounced
division of personality raise the suspicion of a
sexual origin or strong sexual contributing factor,

and the birth of a new personality calling itself by a new name (especially a pet name or nick-name) may in some cases have a partial cause in the common custom of personifying the generative organs and referring to them by a nick-name.

Psychology rejects the doctrine of an "unconscious mind" or "subconscious" because all the empirically observed phenomena on which the mystics seek to base these doctrines are easily explicable on hypotheses which are already in use and which are indispensable to psychology. The conception of *awareness,* whether perceptual or ideational, as a feature of organic reactions, and varying with the reactions, is the key to the understanding of mental processes. With the additions of the law of integration, and the law of the causal connection of successive reactions, neither of which can safely be omitted from modern biology, the basis for the explanation of mental life becomes so complete that the doctrine of "unconscious" mind becomes absurdly superfluous.

Memory is explicable as due to a modification of the nervous system such that the same reaction which produced the modification may occur later; such modification being not a mere hypothesis, but a fact demonstrable in detail from the observable operations of habit. ‚The specific modification on which the memory is based may become obliterated in time: *forgetting* is essentially the same process as the loss of a habit of some other than the ideational kind. Modifications which have for a long time not shown their effects may, under proper circumstances reassert themselves: not only do "memories" thus return, but obviously muscular knacks which apparently have been lost, may be revived.

Modifications of the nervous system which have been produced by conscious reactions may persist, and influence later reactions, both conscious and non-conscious, without the reinstatement of the original conscious processes. This follows from the fundamental mechanics of the nervous system, and is demonstrable in "motor" habits as well as in consciousness. Earlier conscious experiences thus influence later conscious experiences—else education would be impossible—through the nervous mechanism, in a far simpler way than would be required if the original experiences had to be reinstated to secure their effects. My process of handwriting, for example, is a conscious process: the result of long hours of vividly conscious reactions in school. These early experiences have so modified my nervous system that the present process occurs, without the necessity (awful to think upon!) of reviving my school experiences. Nor does it add anything to the explanation to suppose these experiences, in a ghostly form, hovering above the practical operation of the nervous system, in a mystic realm of "unconscious mind" and supervising the process in a way rather disconcerting to the principle of the conservation of energy.

The process of education, we might add, seems to be a process of eliminating consciousness wherever possible. We get the best results from our past experiences when these past experiences have done their work so well that they need not be revived.

The concept of "unconscious mind" is rejected also, when it is ostensibly offered as synonymous with *instinct,* or *habit,* or both, without any specific claim as to its mystic nature. If instinct and habit are meant, it is better to call them by their proper names: there would be no object in substituting for them the terms of "unconscious mind" if there were not the possibility, once the term is adopted, of using it in a sense to mean more than the accurate terms do. The "unconscious mind" or "subconsciousness" when thus offered is the hoary wooden horse perfidiously packed with the ancient enemy of science.

The theory of the "unconscious mind," like the theory of the "third kind of knowledge," evidently results from lack of clear and intelligent analysis, and the painstaking application of hypotheses scientifically founded. The function of scientific psychology is precisely this hard, but profitable, labor, which the mystic shirks. The significant feature of mysticism, which comes strongly to the surface in the Freudian school, is its antipathy to experimentation.

Scientific psychology has also enemies to combat other than the obvious mystics. The world at the present time is seething with spurious psychology of various brands, which is being promoted, in the main, because it profits the promoters financially. Spiritualism, telepathy, "character analysis," "how to develop your mind," "vocational guidance," "business psychology," systems for "memory training," etc., are being exploited in an energetic manner. Various pseudo-psychological systems of healing are reaping a golden harvest. Even the mental tests, painstakingly developed by the psychologists, are beginning to be exploited in a lamentable way, and in certain quarters there is even a definite movement on foot to facilitate the exploitation by legally excluding psychologists from the administration of the tests!

Most of the pseudo-psychological delusions, in so far as they are honestly entertained, are due to ignorance of the nature and method of scientific proof. The evidence for most of the "wild" hypotheses is of the popular or anecdotal nature: "historical" proof at its worst: and disappears when brought under scientific control. It is true, however, that ignorance of fundamental psychological and biological facts is also a large contributing factor in the popular superstitions. "Character analysis," for example, based on the color of the hair and eyes, shape of the nose and mouth, the bumps on the head, or the lines of the palm, is credible only to the person ignorant of the neural basis of mental life, and ignorant of the established laws of heredity.

It is not within the province of this volume to follow the details of the various popular delusions of the day. Such may be a useful labor, but our present purpose is the exposition of the principles through which illusions may be dissipated and truth obtained. A relatively lengthy exposition of the errors of the mystics has been given, not merely because of the gravity of these errors, but also because the exposition serves well to illustrate the clarifying principles of scientific psychology. The application to other pseudo-psychological notions will be a separate labor.

In conclusion, I ask the general reader to bear in mind that much that has been written for popular consumption as "psychology," has no standing among real psychologists, and that the measure of a real psychologist must be derived from the group of men and women officially designated as psychologists by the great institutions of learning and research. There are many genuine psychologists outside these ranks, and there are perhaps a few pseudo-psychologists inside: but the answer to the question whether or not a certain one is a psychologist, and his teachings seriously to be considered, must be checked by comparison with the acknowledged group. Many self-styled psychologists, entirely lacking in scientific training, are unfortunately active; and the statements that "psychologists now admit the existence of the unconscious mind (or telepathy, or some such myth)" or, "an eminent psychologist says (such and such wild theory)" depend on the admissions and sayings of no psychologists at all.

I believe that the overwhelming majority of the recognized psychologists of the United States are already in sympathy with the position, neither unduly radical nor unduly conservative, which is herein designated as *Scientific Psychology*. Some, however, from force of habit, cling to earlier formulations: and some others have gone to unfortunately radical extremes from sheer disgust with the ultraconservatives. Upon all of the profession I urge the consideration of the serious nature of the present situation, and the necessity of uniting on the solid ground of scientific method for the defense of the public welfare against charlatans and teachers of superstition.